Anarchist Accounting

Accounting Principles for
a Participatory Economy

Revised Edition

By Anders Sandström

First published 2016; revised edition 2018 by Glowbox Design Co-op
Copyright © 2016, 2018 Anders Sandström
All rights reserved
ISBN-13: 978-1-326-63483-4
www.anarchistaccounting.info
Cover design & typesetting by Christopher Chrysostomou

www.glowboxdesign.co.uk

"

There currently exist many useless things; many occupations are useless as well, for example, accounting. With anarchy there is no more need for money, no further need for bookkeeping and the other forms of employment that derive from this.

— *Ravachol (late 1800s)*

CONTENTS

Preface	ix

Introduction	1
Anarchist Economics	4
History of Accounting	5
Outline of the book	8

CHAPTER 1
Participatory Economics	11
Goals	12
Institutions	14
Arguments against the market	17
Participatory planning	22

CHAPTER 2
The Actors	33
Consumers	34
Workers	36
Federations and Long Term Planning	38
The Iteration Facilitation Board	40

CHAPTER 3
The Accounting System	41
The general purpose of accounting in a participatory economy	42
Accounting entities and transactions	43
Consumption rights in a participatory economy	66

CHAPTER 4
Consumption	71
Individual consumption and the categorisation of goods and services	72
Consumer accounts, cost centres and their internal relations	75

The physical distribution of goods	80
Trade with second-hand goods	82
Collective consumption	86
Examples of Collective Consumption	90
Housing and community facilities	92

CHAPTER 5
Work and Production — 97

Distribution of consumption points	98
Worker councils' productive capacity	102
The production of goods and services	112

CHAPTER 6
Long-term Planning — 123

Industries and the classification of federations	125
Society's productive capacity	128
Trade with other economies	135

CHAPTER 7
The Environment — 143

CHAPTER 8
Summary — 149

APPENDIX 1:
Accounting Primer — 155

APPENDIX 2:
Inventory and Accruals — 159

APPENDIX 3:
Entries for Collective Consumer Investments — 161

References and Links — 164

PREFACE

The first time I came in contact with the participatory economics model was around the turn of the millennium. At the time I had already walked some distance down the mental road that would lead me away from a rather extreme neoliberal worldview where Margaret Thatcher and Ronald Reagan were role models, to an insight that finally drove me to a radical revaluation and reorientation of, not only my worldview but also of my whole life situation. In my job at the time as head of accounting in a large market leading bus company, I had become well aware of the obvious contempt that senior management at large companies can show towards their employees, and their relentless focus on maximising profit and personal gain at any cost, and above all, I had realised that I myself in my job was part of this. About the same time, mostly by a coincidence, I bought one of Noam Chomsky's books. In Chomsky's books systemic injustice and abuse of power, and their causes, are explained and described so clearly and obviously that it is impossible not to be affected. What an eye-opener it was! Thus my journey had begun.

I quickly became aware that the attempts to establish authoritarian socialist societies made during the twentieth century had been failures and that in practice they were often more undemocratic and unjust than the capitalism they replaced. It was obvious that hierarchies and concentration of power led to injustices and lack of freedom no matter how appealing the pro-worker rhetoric of Communist leaders. Libertarian tendencies within the socialist family of ideas seemed to provide a compelling analysis of the failures of authoritarian socialism.

Somewhere among all the texts on libertarian socialism, guild socialism, syndicalism and anarchism, which I began to read there was a reference to Participatory Economics. The Participatory Economics model was the clearest and most thoughtful alternative economic vision I had encountered. It describes in a coherent and consistent way how a modern society can organise its economy democratically and justly on the basis of libertarian socialist values, without private ownership of capital and without markets.

However, since my background is in accounting, I could not help but start pondering some of the practical accounting problems I felt the model generated that were not answered in any of the presentations of the model that I read. In September 2012 Professor Robin Hahnel, one of the model's two creators, visited Sweden and Stockholm for a number of presentations of the participatory economic model. During one of our informal conversations, I jokingly, but with a shred of seriousness, said that I was thinking about writing a book on accounting principles in a participatory economy. Without any hesitation Robin replied: "Then I have the perfect title ... Anarchist Accounting". The book title was born!

During the summer of 2014, I began writing and taking notes on various accounting problems, and their solutions, that I thought a future participatory economy would inevitably have to deal with. The notes grew and after a while I contacted Jason Chrysostomou, co-founder of the organisation Participatory Economics UK, to ask if he would be interested in helping with the creation of an English version. From this moment the book project became a collaborative effort, the result of which is both an English and a Swedish version of *Anarchist Accounting: Accounting Principles for a Participatory Economy*. I would also like to express my gratitude to others who have helped with designing diagrams, providing feedback and with proof reading. I am especially grateful to Professor Robin Hahnel who has provided extensive and constructive feedback for the book's initial two chapters, which describe the participatory economics model and set the scene for the rest of the book.

The book is essentially my own personal attempt to answer questions regarding the accounting of economic transactions in a participatory economy and I am solely responsible for any shortcomings in the suggested solutions of accounting problems that are presented in the book. Hopefully, others who are interested in serious and realistic alternatives to capitalism, and perhaps above all their practical implementation, will find the arguments interesting and stimulating.

Anders Sandström

Stockholm, 29th February 2016

INTRODUCTION

If they think about it at all, most people assume there is no better alternative than capitalism, i.e. that markets and private ownership of capital are as unchangeable as the laws of nature. The widespread embrace of Margaret Thatcher's old TINA argument (There Is No Alternative) is arguably one of the biggest obstacles to replacing an economic system based on greed and competition with one based on democracy and justice.

People have a right to be sceptical of non-capitalist economic visions in light of twentieth century history[1]. Contemporary visions of a new economic system and a just society must provide an alternative to both capitalism and twentieth century authoritarian socialism. We who are looking for a different society must become much better at presenting and defending our visions, and above all, in explaining how they differ from twentieth century versions. At the same time, there is the risk that vision can promote sectarianism and elitism. To avoid this, and to ensure the right of future generations to make their own decisions, our visions must be flexible, inclusive, and allow continuous adaptation to new information and a changing world.

However, thinking through economic vision in a serious and concrete way provides at least three important benefits: (1) It builds optimism and confidence in the feasibility of a more desirable alternative system, (2) it helps to assess alternative strategic and tactical actions in our everyday struggles, and (3) it helps to inform experiments when people are in a position to begin implementing alternative social institutions. As long as visions are presented as merely proposals or suggestions and not as ideologically rigid dogmas, thinking through potential problems and exploring possible solutions in advance, can only be of help to future citizens who ultimately will decide how to build their new society.

How would accounting and bookkeeping look like in a society that does not allow private equity owners and private lenders and creditors, a society that is not based on greed and competition but instead on cooperation and solidarity? How would capital assets and production units be valued and monitored if they were not owned by private equity owners, and if the allocation of goods and services were not done through markets but instead through a form of democratic planning? Who would

---

1 In *Economic Justice and Democracy: From Competition to Cooperation*, Routledge Books 2005, Robin Hahnel describes twentieth century attempts to replace capitalism, and more contemporary alternative visions that have been created as a reaction to the failures of the twentieth century.

ask for what information? A non-capitalist, democratic economic system will need a coherent set of accounting principles in order to enable those affected by decisions to judge whether resource allocation and distribution of consumption rights is efficient and fair - at least as long as we live in a society with scarce resources.

This book focuses on the economy, and even more specifically on how accounting and bookkeeping principles could be designed in a libertarian socialist economic system. It explores what information and recording of transactions would be necessary to enable democratic participation and efficient decisions by those affected by decisions. The text must not in any way be interpreted as a definitive and immutable description of how the future accounting principles must be designed, but instead as just one of many possible ways to translate values into concrete solutions to technical issues. It should be seen as a starting point for further and ongoing discussions, and as a source of additional thoughts and ideas on the subject.

Some of the accounting terms that are used in the text may seem technical and sometimes even "capitalistic". This is inevitable because there is not yet an alternative non-capitalist economic terminology available to describe accounting principles no matter what system they belong to. A future alternative society is likely to develop a completely different set of terms to describe the activities and relationships discussed in this book. However, we want to show that it is possible to formulate and describe a coherent set of bookkeeping and accounting principles that are compatible with, and may even promote the goals of economic democracy and justice, even now, regardless of the concepts and terms used.

We hope to demystify issues that most consider too technical to concern themselves with, and show that a non-dogmatic discussion can be valuable despite some potential risks. We want to help demonstrate that alternative economic systems are indeed possible, and not merely lofty utopias that cannot be put into practice. And we want to inspire further discussion about economic vision. A discussion of this sort will of course never be "finished" but should constantly adapt and evolve based on new insights and new knowledge in a changing environment.

While this book focuses on the economy, it is important to keep in mind that the economy is only one part of society and that hierarchies with underprivileged and disadvantaged groups are found in all areas of society where the benefits and hardships resulting from social interaction are not distributed equally.[2]

ANARCHIST ECONOMICS

Anarchism is a political philosophy concerned with the abolition of coercive structures of authority and centralised power in society.[3] While today there exists much public misconception that associates anarchism with disorder and chaos, anarchist thinkers throughout the ages had in mind a highly organised form of society in which power, instead of flowing from the top-down, flows from the bottom-up. The closest example of an economy organised along these lines was in Spain from 1933-1936 where large parts of the economy in Republican controlled territory were under worker control, and industries were organised around federations of assemblies consisting of delegates subject to recall.

Participatory Economics is a formal economic model first presented in 1991 in two books by Michael Albert and Robin Hahnel[4], which is influenced by and firmly rooted within the anarchist/libertarian socialist heritage. Since then, it has been discussed, further developed and scrutinised in numerous subsequent books, articles, panel discussions, and debates on various forums all over the internet. The authors attempt to explain in concrete terms how in practice a modern economy of millions of people could be organised around the principles of self-management, equity and solidarity, as an alternative to both capitalism and authoritarian planning. A participatory economy is composed of self-managed worker and consumer councils, their federations, and a decentralised democratic planning procedure, outlined in more detail in the next chapter.

Anarchist Accounting: Accounting Principles for a participatory economy is based on the participatory economics vision but takes an additional step and discusses how accounting and bookkeeping could be designed

---

2 For an account of how society's different spheres, their institutions, and hierarchies affects each other see Michael Albert et al., *Liberating Theory*, South End Press, 1986.

3 For a good overview on anarchist thought see Daniel Guerin. Anarchism. Monthly Review Press 1970 and Noam Chomsky. *On anarchism*. AK Press 2014.

4 Michael Albert and Robin Hahnel. *Looking forward*, South End Press 1991 and Michael Albert and Robin Hahnel. *The Political Economy of Participatory Economics*, Princeton University Press 1991.

and performed in a future libertarian socialist economy, in a way that is both consistent with and promotes its core values. This book is based on the Participatory Economics model and focuses on the model's institution for allocation - participatory planning - and especially on the requirements that participatory planning poses on information requirements and accounting. It touches only superficially and indirectly on the models other institutions such as jobs balanced for empowerment and desirability, and democratic decision-making procedures within the self-managed councils.

HISTORY OF ACCOUNTING

Every economy, both today and in the future, needs and will need some form of accounting. Accounting is the registration, summarisation and reporting of economic transactions in order to provide the necessary information for making economic decisions. For those unfamiliar with the subject, in Appendix 1 we provide a short introduction to accounting, which we recommend reading first.

The development of financial accounting from the simple notes of commercial transactions in antiquity to today's comprehensive accounting systems for monitoring, managing and controlling economic activity is the result of the needs of those in power and of capital owners, their need for increasingly sophisticated accounting procedures in order to maximise their return on investments and to administer and control trade, credit and production in different historical eras. The development and design of accounting systems have, in turn, influenced how and how quickly different economic systems and ideologies have developed, by creating favourable conditions for a certain type of capital accumulation through effective monitoring and control of economic activities. The growing complexity of accounting systems has also enabled the bookkeepers throughout history and especially in recent years to monopolise accounting knowledge, and to form themselves as an independent group of professionals with their own aspirations of power and influence in relation to their property owning principles.[5]

---

5   Our short summary of the historic development of accounting is based on two texts: An article by Certified Public Accountant Stefan Engström in the Swedish magazine Balans #12/99, and H. Thomas Johnson and Robert S. Kaplan. *Relevance Lost. The Rise and Fall of Management Accounting*. Harvard Business School Press. 1987.

The cradle of financial accounting is usually placed in Mesopotamia, in the area around the Tigris and Euphrates rivers in present Iraq over 5,000 years ago. Favourable circumstances in that area gave rise to relatively developed trade. Several major trade centres such as Babylon and Nineveh came into existence, and a fledgling banking system began to take shape, which provided loans to merchants. Thus arose also the need to keep records and to control trade and debt transactions. But it was not until the early Middle Ages that what is referred to as modern accounting, i.e. double entry bookkeeping, arose. It is believed that the system of double-entry bookkeeping emerged in the Italian banks in city-states such as Florence and Venice in the 1200s where bank customers were assigned accounts with both deposits and liabilities. Transfers of money between people with accounts in the same bank could then easily be recorded by a simultaneous listing of the current balance on separate accounts with two sides or columns (Debit and Credit) which identified deposits and liabilities. In 1494 the Venice based Franciscan monk Luca Pacioli created the first known description in writing of double entry accounting in the mathematical dissertation *Summa de Arithmetica Geometria Proportioni et Proportionalita* (Overview of arithmetic, geometry, rule of three and proportionality).

Before the industrial revolution the purpose of bookkeeping was mainly to register transactions between independent producers of goods and their customers, or traders who bought goods for resale, or between lenders and borrowers. During the seventeenth and eighteenth centuries large trading companies were created, such as the East India Company, which ran an extensive trade in colonies around the world where the focus was on trade with exotic goods from distant parts of the world. Profits were the result of buying "exotic" goods cheap in the colonies and selling them dear in the home country, combined with buying manufactured goods cheap in the home country and selling them dear in the colonies. The actual production of goods in both colonies and home countries was carried out largely independently by peasants and artisans who largely controlled the actual production process. The pricing of goods and assets from an accounting perspective was simple and followed naturally as a result of market transactions between independent parties. With the industrial revolution an entirely different scenario came into play.

In the early nineteenth century technical progress had made it possible and profitable to mass produce goods. It became profitable for the owners of capital to invest much larger sums in production than before. Workers were contracted for longer time and it became important and significant to control and manage production processes. A hierarchical work division and organisation grew rapidly, with groups of workers whose only job was to manage and control other workers. The production units grew ever larger as a result of better and more efficient ways of communication and economies of scale, and it became important for investors to evaluate and compare different units based on the most profitable use of scarce resources. A large number of economic indicators and analytical tools were developed to evaluate and compare the efficiency of different units with respect to hours worked, resources used, etc. This trend was intensified by Taylorism which, in the early twentieth century, attempted to scientifically determine the optimal use of materials and labour. A growing proportion of transactions in time became internal transactions within large organisations and between different organisational units within the same group. Early in the twentieth century senior officials in the multinational DuPont Group[6] developed a set of key indicators or key ratios in order to facilitate the allocation of capital to the most profitable units within the Group – the so-called "Return On Investment" (ROI) ratios. Different versions of ROI ratios are still widely used today.

After the Second World War and especially in the period after 1970 the world economy has been characterised by two strong trends; an increasing concentration of capital and ownership in most industries, and an expanding financial sector. Many industries today are dominated by a small number of global and very large business groups that are often inter-linked and whose revenues in many cases exceed the GDPs of smaller countries. These business groups often control and own actors in several stages in the production and distribution chain. At the same time speculative financial transactions make up an overwhelming majority of all monetary transactions in today's economy. Many companies nowadays make significantly more money by speculating in currencies and securities than by producing goods and services and providing them to consumers. Furthermore, the principles of accounting for many of

---

6 The DuPont Company was founded in 1802 producing gunpowder. Early on it diversified its production into different chemical products. Today it is one of the world's largest companies in its industry.

today's innovative financial securities are often impenetrable and it is very difficult to get an accurate idea of these financial assets' values.

Today's accounting principles emerged and were shaped by the interests of private capital owners in controlling and managing the use of their capital, by nation states' interest in taxing corporations profits and assets, and by demands from accountants who in their daily work prepare financial information in income statements, balance sheets, cash flow reports, financial analyses, etc. While all accounting systems will inevitably share some common characteristics, differences in any future accounting system will reflect the differences in the economy's key institutions regarding the ownership of capital, its allocation system, modes of compensation, division of labour, etc.

OUTLINE OF THE BOOK

While this is a book on accounting and is therefore unavoidably somewhat technical in nature, every attempt has been made to make it as accessible as possible to non-accountants. Tables, diagrams and examples have been added throughout where possible to aid comprehension. Nevertheless, some sections do require some prior basic accounting knowledge. However, we are confident that readers with curious minds who are interested in exploring more practical matters around the organisation of a libertarian socialist economy, but who have no background in accounting, will still gain value from reading the book. Furthermore, since the book is based on the participatory economics model, the more knowledge one has of this model the better.

The first chapter gives a brief summary of the participatory economics vision, its values and institutions, as well as the main arguments against the market as an allocation mechanism. The chapter focuses on the model's institution for allocation - decentralised participatory planning - and its procedures. Participatory planning is a decentralised democratic planning procedure based on self-management in which it is the consumers and the producers themselves who propose and revise their own consumption and production.

In the second chapter we identify more carefully the actors and decision makers in a participatory economy, and identify and categorise the most important decisions and the demands on information and monitoring that different decision situations pose. In chapter three we then briefly summarise the main overall objectives that an accounting system would have in a participatory economy and how the accounting system can be designed to achieve these objectives. The bulk of the chapter is devoted to providing a schematic picture of how economic transactions in a participatory economy could be recorded and monitored.

In chapter four, we focus on consumption - both private and public – and the tasks that consumers perform, and the information they need. It is the consumers themselves, and not some central planning unit, that announce their consumption preferences in a participatory economy so that the worker councils can plan their production accordingly. This task must be possible to perform in a way that is not too detailed, and therefore too cumbersome and time-consuming for consumers. How "coarse" and flexible can consumers' consumption plans be, and what information do consumers need to be able to judge whether their own and others' consumption proposals are fair or not? Furthermore, the accounting system needs to be able to record and compare consumers' incomes and expenses, allow for loans and savings, and manage deviations between planned and actual outcomes in a flexible and equitable manner.

Chapter five focuses on work and production. We first discuss possible principles for the allocation of income *between* worker councils and how well these principles reflect differences in council members' effort or sacrifices. We do not address the internal allocation of consumption rights between individual members *within* a workers council. We then concentrate on how worker councils get access to production capacity and the pricing of user rights for different productive resources - i.e. produced capital, natural resources, intermediate goods, and labour. The pricing of user rights for productive resources should reflect differences in resources' productivity, which requires a categorisation of the resources that allows for this to happen. We then move on to discuss the categorisation of the goods and services that the worker councils produce using the productive resources they have access to.

The sixth chapter describes investment planning and long-term development planning. We discuss the classification and organisation of worker councils into industry federations and the basis on which such classification can be made, and what responsibilities the industry federations have. We move on to look at the planning of the productive capacity development of different industries, which results in specific and detailed investment plans. In addition, industry federations need to establish and fund various shared support function units in order to implement, monitor and evaluate the agreed investment plans. The supplies of different kinds of labour also need to be adjusted in light of long term development decisions and we discuss how this can be done. Finally, we look at trade between different economies and discuss the basis on which international trade should be organised.

Chapter seven, the last chapter before the summary, describes how the social costs created by emissions of polluting substances can be handled in a way that is based on a participatory economy's basic values. It is the preferences of the parties who are affected by pollution – whom we call the "communities of affected parties", or CAPs - that should form the basis for the pricing of emissions of polluting substances. The parties who are adversely affected by pollutants should have the right to decide whether they want to prohibit a substance altogether or receive compensation for the damage it causes them when released, and the parties that cause damage by polluting should be charged for the damage caused.

CHAPTER 1

PARTICIPATORY ECONOMICS

In this chapter we provide an overview of the model of a participatory economy[7] and try to convey a sense of its fundamental values and an understanding of the model's defining institutions. For those who want to immerse themselves further, we recommend a visit to the website *www.participatoryeconomics.info* which includes links to further articles, videos, books and other resources.

GOALS

Any economy has three tasks to accomplish: the organisation of 1) production and 2) consumption, and because humans abandoned individual economic self-sufficiency long ago in order to take advantage of the efficiency gains from a division of labour, 3) the allocation of goods, services, and resources among different producers, users, and consumers. A participatory economy, while performing these three tasks, explicitly aims to advance six specific goals: economic democracy, economic justice, solidarity, diversity, efficiency and ecological sustainability.

Economic Democracy

Supporters of the participatory economics vision define economic democracy as a condition where a person's influence over decisions is determined by how much the person is affected by the decision in question. If you are affected more than others by a decision, you should have more influence over that decision; if you are less affected than others by a decision, you should have less influence. This is also called self-management, which is the only way to promote economic freedom without the freedoms of some disenfranchising the freedoms of others.

Economic Justice

Economic justice is about the distribution of the benefits and burdens that result from economic activity. In a participatory economy the goal is for any differences in income, i.e. a person's share of what is produced in the economy, to be based on differences in sacrifices or personal effort in performing socially valuable work. Income distribution should not be affected by how productive one's labour is, due to having access to

---

7 For a longer and excellent presentations of the model see R. Hahnel, *Of the People, By the People: The Case for a Participatory Economy*, Soapbox Press, 2012.

better tools and capital, being born with a higher intelligence or other factors that are beyond a person's control. Effort and personal sacrifice are the only factors that a person can influence and thus form the main basis on which any differences in compensation should be based. Of course, there are also many circumstances when income should be distributed based on need. For example, when people are not able to work because of severe disability; are too young or old to work, i.e. children and senior citizens; when in need of health and social care during times of illness; if they become victims of natural disasters, and in many other situations, as decided democratically by society. The complete rule for distribution of income or consumption possibilities in a participatory economy is therefore "to each according to effort or personal sacrifice, and needs".

Solidarity

Solidarity is defined here as concern for others' well-being and the attitude that circumstances for our fellow human beings should be valued and assessed as if they were our own. In private enterprise economies the interests of employers and employees are opposed to one another. And in market economies buyers and sellers are pitted against each other such that success for one person is achieved at the expense of someone else. A participatory economy seeks to create an environment where mutual aid, cooperation and solidarity is encouraged, and where our interests are intertwined in a way that the individual success means that others benefit as well.

Diversity

Diversity refers to a situation where people have access to a large number of different choices about how to meet their needs and desires. People vary greatly regarding their preferences, tastes, talents and lifestyles; the best life for one person is not necessarily the best life for another. A participatory economy therefore rejects conformity in favour of a society characterised by a great deal of diversity. An additional benefit of promoting diversity is the spreading of risks; it is advantageous to allow and test many ideas and options in different areas. That way, more doors will be kept open, and experience and knowledge will increase.

Efficiency

Efficiency means that our goals are achieved with the least possible waste of resources, time, effort and energy. A participatory economy wants to maximise human well-being for all, which requires using scarce resources where they are most valuable.

Ecological Sustainability

These five goals already indirectly supporting ecological sustainability, but supporters of participatory economics see long-term sustainability and the concern for the environment as an important and independent value in and of itself. A participatory economy is a green economy that wants to achieve economic goals without diminishing future generations' access to a stimulating and rewarding natural environment.

INSTITUTIONS

The next step is to consider how these goals will be achieved. The participatory economics model defines a minimal set of institutions designed to maximise our potential for achieving the above objectives. These institutions are; democratic worker and consumer councils, jobs where tasks are "balanced" with regard to empowerment, and where possible desirability; compensation based on effort or sacrifice and needs, and finally, a democratic allocation process, called participatory planning.

Democratic worker and consumer councils

In a participatory economy the means of production such as land, natural resources, factories, machinery and technical knowledge are owned collectively by all. All of this is treated as the "productive commons," belonging no more to any person than anyone else. Influence over decisions is therefore not based on ownership of private property, or on different groups' bargaining power. Instead, people meet in democratic worker and consumer councils and their respective federations, where they discuss and vote on decisions regarding their own affairs. All members have equal rights and all members have one vote.

The worker council is the highest decision-making body in every workplace in the same manner as the annual shareholder general meeting is, in theory, the highest decision-making body in a corporation in today's economic system. In addition, decision-making in every workplace should be organised to maximise self-management, i.e. so that each worker can influence decisions in proportion to the degree that she or he is affected by the outcome of the decision. To achieve this, different voting procedures can be agreed on to be used in different situations within workplaces, such as majority vote, consensus or different types of qualified majority. Larger workplaces may decide to create semi-autonomous subdivisions with decision-making authority over matters that primarily affect only them. All are free to apply for membership in the worker councils of their choice, or to apply to start a new worker council.

Each individual also belongs to a local neighbourhood consumer council. The consumer councils, among other things, handle individual household's requests for consumption, i.e. their suggested list of goods and services they wish to consume during the following year. An individual consumer's consumption rights are constrained by the member's income that she is allocated in her workplace (based on effort or sacrifice), in addition to any income she may receive through internal redistribution within consumer councils (based on need) or via the national system for allocation of income to those who are too young to work, retired or disabled. Every individual consumes both private goods such as food and clothing, and public goods such as parks, libraries and playgrounds. Through their neighbourhood consumer councils, and through delegates to higher level federations of consumer councils, consumers propose collective consumption at the same time that they make their requests for private consumption.

Every worker and consumer council elects representatives to the "higher" levels of councils, called council federations. Worker council federations are organised by industry and consumer council federations are organised geographically in increasingly larger geographic areas. For example, by neighbourhood, city, region and national level. This structure is necessary because different kinds of collective consumption, or public goods, affect smaller and larger constituencies. In order to counteract any potential misuse of power, representatives acting within federations can be subject to rules of rotation, recall and instructions from members of the council at lower levels.

Balanced jobs

In any economy, there are jobs that define the tasks a worker has to perform. In hierarchically organised economies such as capitalism or centrally planned state socialism the majority of jobs are defined in such a way that most of the tasks in a particular job are *either* relatively empowering *or* disempowering. This leads to a situation where a minority will monopolise access and utilisation of information and knowledge in the workplace, which in turn leads to a situation whereby this group dominates meetings and discussions in the workplace due to greater confidence and knowledge, even in a situation where every worker formally has one vote. An uneven distribution of empowering tasks promotes class differences and hierarchies.

A participatory economy aims to organise work in a radically different way in order to achieve real influence for everyone in the workplace and in society at large. To the degree that it is possible every workplace is expected to combine tasks into jobs that are roughly comparable in terms of empowering tasks. This means that all workers perform some tasks that are empowering and some that are less so. The idea is not that everyone should perform every task in a workplace. There will still be specialisation. A balanced job will still contain a limited number of tasks but at least some will be empowering, and tasks that are not empowering will be part of everyone's job. Balancing jobs for empowerment will help equip all in a workplace to participate meaningfully in democratic decision-making.

Every worker council is responsible for balancing jobs to the extent possible, and the way they approach this will necessarily vary greatly between different workplaces, depending on different practical, technological, and individual considerations.

Compensation based on effort, sacrifice, and need

A worker receives consumption rights, (or in other words, income), as compensation for work performed. In our current economy, the size of an individual's income depends on a variety of factors such as ownership of capital, bargaining power, talent, education, luck, and to a much lesser extent, effort or sacrifice. Because the only one of these factors a person can influence is their effort, a participatory economy aims to compensate workers based on the effort and personal sacrifice that they put into (socially valuable) work.

Worker councils are required to establish procedures *of their choosing* for grading members' efforts. Workers who choose to put in a higher level of effort in their work will receive more income. Effort or sacrifice can take different forms, such as working longer hours, working at a higher intensity, or performing more dangerous or unhealthy tasks. How worker councils evaluate effort is up to them, and they are likely to design very different procedures for this purpose. The only restriction is that the worker council's average effort rating, or consumption points that it distributes to its members is capped. Either every workplace is capped with the same average number of points it can distribute to its members, or alternatively this cap can be based on the relationship between the social benefit of the "outputs" the workplace produced in the previous year compared to the social cost of the "inputs" that the workplace used. This will be explained in detail later in the book. The purpose of putting a cap on the average effort ratings a workplace can assign to its members is to avoid the possibility that workers would deliberately exaggerate one another's efforts leading to "inflation" in consumption points.

Finally, decisions about awarding consumption rights based on special circumstances and needs on compassionate grounds are handled in the consumer councils, and decisions about consumption allowances due to disability, retirement and youth – both with regard to rules for eligibility and how large the allowances should be – are handled through a national system within the national consumption federation, not within workplaces.

ARGUMENTS AGAINST THE MARKET[8]

Before describing the final "defining" institution of a participatory economy - participatory planning - it may be worth thinking about why the market (a system of competitive bidding between individual buyers and sellers) is an undesirable allocation mechanism for a participatory economy. What are the arguments against the market?

Here we briefly present four arguments against retaining the market system: Markets (1) are unjust, (2) undermine solidarity and promote selfish attitudes and behaviours, (3) undermine both economic and political democracy, and finally (4) allocate scarce resources inefficiently.

---

8   This section on arguments against the market is a summary of the arguments Robin Hahnel delivered before the Ministry for the Communal Economy in Venezuela during a visit in 2007. See www.monthlyreview.org/2008/01/01/against-the-market-economy-advice-to-venezuelan-friends/

Markets are unfair

In a private enterprise market economy capital owners receive compensation in the form of profit without exerting any work effort, meaning that the benefits that employees collectively receive are necessarily less than the market value of what they produced. Most socialists regard this to be unfair. But what about the income differences between categories of workers, and what if capitalist enterprises are replaced by worker-owned companies that take on members from a labour market where supply and demand is allowed to continue to influence relative wages? When labour is hired through a labour market - regardless of ownership - those who make a greater contribution to the companies' production and income (i.e. those who possess more "human capital") will obtain a higher income than those who contribute to revenues to a lesser extent (those who possess less "human capital") regardless of their effort and sacrifices. This is not consistent with our goal of economic justice, as explained above. Moreover, there is no way to correct this problem within the framework of the market system without creating large inefficiencies. If through legislation we set the salary levels that we believe to be just but continue to allow the market to allocate resources, different types of labour will be allocated inefficiently and the price structure in the whole economy will give inaccurate information about the social costs of producing various goods and services, which leads to further inefficiency.[9]

Markets undermines solidarity and promote selfishness

Disgust with the commercialisation of human relations is as old as trade itself. Markets encourage forms of human interaction that are characterised by pettiness and enmity while forms of cooperation based on respect and empathy are discouraged. Markets reward the most effective exploitation of fellow human beings and punish those who (without logic) insist on following the "golden rule" - treating others as you want to be treated. We are told that in a market system we will benefit by being useful to others but it is usually much easier to gain much greater benefits by exploiting others. Thoughtfulness, empathy and solidarity become unnecessary appendages in market economies.

---

9 In the e-book *Alternatives to Capitalism: Proposals for a Democratic Economy'*, Verso Books 2015, Robin Hahnel and Erik Olin Wright discuss pros and cons of participatory economics and a variant of market socialism.

Markets have important political and cultural effects. Anthropologists point out that the way in which we regulate and coordinate our trade and economic activities affects the type of people we become, and markets are social environments that nurture callousness while punishing solidarity. As much as economists insist on ignoring it, the economy - its markets, workplaces etc. - is a gigantic school with rewards that encourage the development of specific skills and attitudes while other potential abilities and attitudes atrophy.

Markets are undemocratic.

First, markets undermine the character traits and abilities that are necessary for the democratic process. Among the abilities that those who have studied the issue believe to be fundamental to a well-functioning democracy is the ability to manage and communicate complex information, to take collective decisions, and the ability to feel empathy and solidarity with others. Markets create a hostile environment for the cultivation of all these traits. For example, solidarity is more likely to flourish if economic relations are personal and ongoing, rather than anonymous and fleeting as in market economies, and where caring for the needs of others is an integral part of the institutions that govern the economy. In short, the abilities required by the modern, democratic citizen regarding information management and decision-making are not cultivated by participation in market exchange. In fact, these skills and attitudes are undermined by markets.

Second, market transactions generally favour those with more wealth more than those with less capital assets. As long as capital is a scarce resource - i.e. as long as additional capital helps to make someone's work more productive - it is those who hold capital who will receive most of the efficiency gain that market exchanges can create, irrespective of how competitive or non-competitive particular markets happen to be. Economic liberalism and deregulation leads to greater concentration of wealth and, in a political system where money influences electoral prospects, therefore contributes to concentration of political power as well.

Additionally, because markets place pressures on workplaces to cut their costs in order to compete on price with other firms they encourage firms to externalise costs on society and introduce hierarchical decision-making structures within workplaces where senior managers make 'tough' decisions to the detriment of ordinary workers claiming such actions are necessary to keep the firm 'competitive'.

Markets are inefficient.
Economists use two definitions of efficiency. The narrower definition means that an outcome is efficient if there is no other possible outcome where at least one person is better off without someone else being worse off. This is called a Pareto optimal outcome. The broader definition says that a result is efficient if it maximises the net social benefit, i.e. the difference between the total benefit to society and the total cost to society. Based on either of these definitions, all competent economists acknowledge that markets allocate resources inefficiently whenever (a) there are externalities (b) competition is weak, and (c) markets are out of equilibrium.

1) *External effects.* Various manipulations to "externalise" costs, and let others bear the costs of production, and to "internalise" benefits i.e. to assimilate benefits without paying for them, are standard behaviour for companies in a market economy. In so doing they serve their private interest but at the expense of the interests of society. When the seller or buyer promote their own interests by externalising costs to someone who is not a party to the market transaction, or by assimilating benefits from other parties without paying for them, their behaviour creates inefficiencies that lead to misallocation of productive resources and thus to a reduction in economic wellbeing. As a result markets predictably lead to overproduction of goods and services when there are negative externalities associated with their production or consumption, and underproduction of goods and services when there are positive externalities associated with their production or consumption. The same aspect that make market transactions convenient for the buyer and seller – excluding all other affected parties from negotiations – is also a major source of inefficiency.

Those who pay for these externalised costs, so-called "third parties", and thereby increase the private benefits of the buyer and seller are easy victims for two reasons. They are geographically and chronologically scattered, and the negative impact on every individual is small and varies from individual to individual. This means that each individual external party has little incentive to insist on influence over the transaction. It is very difficult and cumbersome to organise coalitions that represent the collective interests when large numbers of people affected are scattered geographically and chronologically and have small but unequal interests at stake. However, the total sum of all external parties' interests are often much larger than the buyer's and seller's interests. One can say that markets reduce transaction costs for buyers and sellers precisely by disenfranchising externally affected stakeholders in the decision-making process.

Today most mainstream economists acknowledge the existence of externalities but usually insist that their effects are small and that they only appear to a limited extent, and therefore they can be disregarded when analysing how efficient markets are and how they function. In reality most, if not all economic transactions affect many people beyond the buyer and seller. In truth, the presence of externalities is the rule, and it is their absence that is the exception.

2) Absence of competition. Markets that are not competitive lead to an inefficient allocation of resources. When there are only a few sellers in a market it is in their interest to produce less than is socially efficient. Most products are currently sold in markets with limited or poorly functioning competition, and the trend is toward less competition, not more. This means that markets with limited competition is an important and growing source of inefficiency in today's market economies.

3) Imbalances between supply and demand. Markets often fail to balance supply and demand. The so-called "laws" of supply and demand which say that the quantity supplied will increase and the quantity demanded will decrease when the market price goes up is based on a highly questionable assumption about how market participants interpret price changes. The standard analysis implicitly assumes that buyers and sellers will see the new higher market price after a price increase as the new stable market price. If this is indeed the case then it is reasonable for sellers to provide more goods than before when the market price rises, and for buyers to demand less than before - in accordance with the law of supply and the law of demand. But sometimes buyers and sellers interpret price changes as an indication of further changes to come in the same direction. This is very common in property, stock and currency markets, but can and does happen in many other markets as well. In which case it is rational for buyers to react to a price increase by increasing the quantity demanded before the price rises even further, and for sellers to reduce the quantities they offer to sell in anticipation of higher prices. When buyers and sellers behave in this way, they create a larger excess demand and drive up the price even higher, leading to a "market bubble". When buyers and sellers interpret a price reduction as an indication of continued price reductions it is rational for buyers to reduce the quantity they demand and wait for even lower prices, and for sellers to increase the quantity they offer to sell before the price drops even more. Their behaviour creates in this case even greater excess supply driving prices down even lower, leading to a "market crash". In other words, if market participants interpret price changes as signals indicating the likely direction of further price changes, and if they act rationally, they will behave contrary to how the "laws" of supply and demand predict, and drive markets even further away from their equilibrium, increasing economic inefficiency.

Is there reason to be optimistic about the possibilities of "taming" markets to mitigate all these inefficiencies? Those who have such hopes downplay the practical problems that inevitably arise when we try to "socialise" markets. Intervention in the form of "Pigovian taxes and subsidies" to correct for externalities would have to be far too extensive. Moreover, since markets do not provide any signals about how high such taxes and subsidies should be, adjustments would inevitably be inadequate. Furthermore, interested parties would have every reason to challenge studies attempting to accurately estimate the true magnitude of external effects. And finally, powerful corporations will oppose breaking up and eliminating non-competitive market structures which generate social inefficiency but are highly profitable.

PARTICIPATORY PLANNING

What is the alternative to markets in a participatory economy? Here we briefly describe the main features of participatory planning[10] - an annual cooperative planning procedure used for the allocation of resources in a participatory economy.

Coordination of economic relations among producers and consumers in a participatory economy is done via a unique democratic planning

---

10 In *The Political Economy of Participatory Economics*, Princeton University Press, 1991 Michael Albert and Robin Hahnel describe the participatory planning in detail using mathematical expressions and equations for an intended audience of trained economists. For a more accessible but still thorough explanation of participatory planning, see *ZNet 2010: Anarchist Planning for The Twenty First Century*: (www.zcomm.org/znetarticle/anarchist-planning-for-twenty-first-century-economies-a-proposal-by-robin-hahnel/), *the Institute for Anarchist Studies: Anarchist Planning: An Interview with Robin Hahnel* by Chris Spannos. (anarchiststudies.mayfirst.org/node/432), and chapter 14 in *Of the People, by the People: The case for a participatory economy*.

procedure called participatory planning, whereby self-managed worker and consumer councils and federations propose and revise their own production and consumption plans, over a number of iterations which gradually leads to a viable, efficient, and equitable plan. The annual planning procedure takes place in light of a previously approved long term development plan and a five year investment plan. This means that the supply of various categories of productive capital and labour that is available for use, and the amount of different capital goods that will be produced in a particular year are known, or "given," when the annual planning process begins. These long term decisions are handled in separate investment planning and development planning procedures that are described in Chapter 6.

The main participants in the planning procedures are the worker councils and their federations, the consumer councils and their federations, and an iteration facilitation board. The workers in the worker councils formulate and adjust their production proposals for the coming year in much the same way as today's companies prepare budgets. They also elect representatives to industry federations. Members of the neighbourhood consumer councils prepare and adjust their household consumption proposals and submit these to neighbourhood council, where they also participate in discussions about what local public goods they want to ask for, and elect recallable representatives to higher level consumer federations.

The Iteration Facilitation Board (IFB) consists of workers whose job it is to facilitate the flow of information during the planning process. The IFB's main task is to update indicative prices - estimates of opportunity costs of using different kinds of productive capital, natural resources and labour, and the social costs of producing intermediate and final goods and services - based on a set of agreed rules for price adjustments before every new planning iteration until a coherent, or "feasible" plan is reached. The workers at the IFB are not central planning bureaucrats who control or make decisions about production or consumption. Besides disseminating non-quantitative information that may be of interest to councils and federations, the only function of workers at the IFB is to update indicative prices between rounds of the planning procedure, and they could, in principle, be replaced by a calculation algorithm.

The steps in the annual participatory planning procedure are simple: Workers suggest what they want to produce; consumers suggest what they want to consume; indicative prices are updated based on excess supply or demand; and the steps are repeated in a number of iterations until a feasible plan is achieved, i.e. until there no longer exists any excess supply or demand for any product or service in the economy. Each round in the planning process consists of the following steps:

Step 1: *Indicative prices are announced*

The IFB announces "indicative prices" which are simply the current estimates of the opportunity costs of using different categories of capital goods, natural resources, and labour; current estimates of the social costs of producing different intermediate and final goods and services; and current estimates of the damages caused by release of different pollutants. "Indicative prices" are, in other words, estimates of what it costs society when we use different resources, emit different pollutants, and produce various goods and services.

Step 2: *Proposals from workplaces and consumers*

Based on the indicative prices consumer councils and federations prepare suggestions regarding what goods and services - both private and collective - they wish to consume. The worker councils prepare proposals for goods and services that they want to produce, and what natural and labour resources, capital goods, and intermediate goods they plan to use in their production. Note that all of these suggestions from worker and consumer councils and federations only refer to their own activities, not to what other workers and consumers should or should not do.

Step 3: *Indicative prices are updated*

The IFB adjusts the indicative prices up or down in proportion to the degree of excess supply or demand.

These three steps are repeated until excess demands are eliminated and a feasible plan is reached. It has been demonstrated[11] that under standard assumptions about technologies and preferences each iteration will generate more accurate estimates of opportunity and social costs, and eventually excess demands and supplies will be eliminated resulting in a feasible plan.

---

11 Michael Albert and Robin Hahnel. *The Political Economy of Participatory Economics*, Princeton University Press 1991.

Who approves the proposals?

Worker councils' production proposals and consumer councils' consumption proposals must be approved by the other councils and federations, which simply vote for or against approving the proposals. But on what basis do councils decide to approve or reject other councils' proposals? The participatory planning procedure is designed with the aim to generate just the information needed in order for workers and consumers to easily be able to assess whether or not other worker councils' production proposals make use of scarce resources in a responsible and efficient manner, and whether or not other consumers' consumption proposals are fair.

In order to evaluate a consumption proposal the total social cost of the proposed consumption is compared with the consumers' consumption points (income). The effort ratings that workers receive in their work places are converted into consumption points which will be explained later in the book. The social cost is calculated simply by multiplying the quantity demanded of each final good and service multiplied by its indicative price, and summing. The consumption points are the points members have earned in their workplaces, been granted because they qualify for consumption rights under programs for youth, retired, and disabled, received in compensation for damages suffered from pollutants, and possibly been granted due to special needs. If the average consumption points of members of a consumer council meet society's average, they will be able to consume goods and services which cost society an

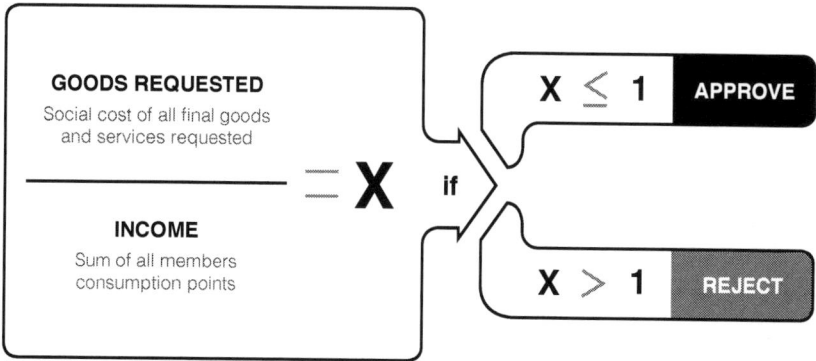

Figure 1.1. Decision making rule for consumption proposals

average amount per person. Consumer councils, whose members have made greater efforts and sacrifices in their workplaces, or have more consumption points from other sources than the average, will be able to consume goods and services whose costs are higher than average, and the councils whose members have less consumption points than average will only be able to consume goods and services that cost society less than the average per person.

On the production side worker councils' production proposals are evaluated by comparing the estimated benefits to society of the goods and services they propose to produce with the opportunity cost of using the capital goods, natural resources, and labour, as well as the social cost of producing the intermediate goods they are asking for. These social benefits and costs are calculated using current indicative prices for all outputs and inputs, including negative indicative prices for proposed emission of pollutants. In this way a social benefit to cost ratio (SB/SC) can be calculated for every worker council proposal. If the SB/SC ratio is greater than one then the proposed use of resources - that belong to everyone in society - is "socially responsible", and all would benefit from approving the proposal. If the ratio is less than one, the proposed use of resources is not efficient because there are other workers who would use the resources more efficiently.

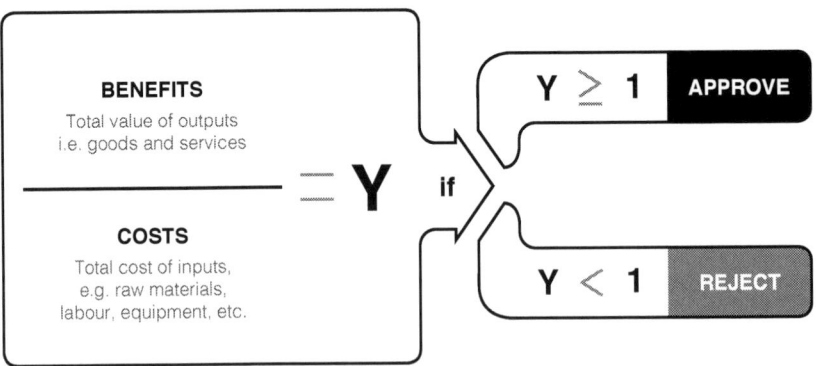

Figure 1.2. Decision making rule for production proposals

The information generated during the planning procedure as described above makes it easy for consumer councils and federations to assess whether their own and others' proposals are fair or not, and for worker councils and their industry federations to assess whether their own and others' proposals are efficient or not, and whether they therefore should approve other councils' proposals or not. Most proposals can easily be approved or rejected, but in some cases, a closer monitoring is justified because it is not always possible to rely on the numbers alone. Worker councils who do not reach an SB/SC ratio larger than one might want to get their proposals examined in more detail, and have an opportunity to argue for their proposals and explain why they do not show better numbers. Therefore, industry federations may establish special audit committees that review some proposals more carefully and make recommendations for approval or rejection.

INDIVIDUAL AND COLLECTIVE CONSUMPTION

Public goods are goods which are consumed collectively by groups of people in neighbourhoods, cities, and even larger geographical units. Examples of collective or public goods are mass transit systems, libraries, parks, and schools. The cost of goods that are consumed collectively are usually borne jointly by the persons in the group which means that their potential for individual consumption is reduced when public consumption is increased. One of the participatory planning procedure's unique characteristics compared to other allocation systems is that consumer preferences for collective consumption can be registered as easy as people's preferences for individual consumption through the consumer councils and their federations.

In the neighbourhood consumer councils members meet to discuss, propose and vote on the level and composition of the councils' collective consumption. A neighbourhood consumer council also sends representatives to federations that cover larger geographical areas and which manage collective consumption for these larger areas. This takes place for increasingly larger geographic areas all the way up to the national level where requests for spending on national public goods like national defence are made. Delegates at these different levels meet, discuss and decide democratically how much and what forms of collective consumption to propose in each planning iteration. It is worth repeating that these meetings only deal with "internal" consumption, i.e. with the councils' and federations' own consumption, and are not concerned with what others should or should not consume.

REACHING A PLAN

All actors that have been approved by their federations to submit proposals can participate in the iterations, without any formal restrictions on their proposals. This includes "aspiring" worker councils that want to get access to productive resources that other worker councils presently use, since they believe they can use these resources more efficiently. After a number of rounds, the final worker councils that will get access to society's productive resources in the coming year will have been established.

The participatory planning procedure promotes efficiency and equity, and leads to a viable, efficient and equitable plan, in two ways. First, consumers who propose an "unfair" consumption i.e. a larger consumption than their income permit, must either reduce their consumption or choose products that are less costly for worker councils to produce to get their consumption plans approved by other consumers. Secondly, worker councils who submit production proposals that are not "efficient", i.e. where the benefits to society of production is less than the social cost, must either increase its efforts or refocus the production so that they produce more products and services that are in demand, or use less costly inputs in order to increase their SB/SC ratio and thereby get other worker councils to approve their proposals. If a proposal is rejected by the other councils it is always the council who submitted the proposal, and no one else, that is responsible for revising the proposal for the next iteration in the planning procedure. This unique aspect distinguishes participatory planning from all other planning models and is crucial in order for "self-management" to be meaningful.

ISSUES TO CONSIDER

After each round of proposals and price adjustments the indicative prices move closer to more accurate estimates of opportunity costs for different categories of capital and labour, damages caused by different pollutants and the social costs for intermediate and final goods and services. The logic behind the IFB's adjustments of indicative prices before each new iteration is simple and could in principle be performed using a mathematical algorithm. However, there is reason to believe that allowing IFB workers some discretion in price adjustment may help reduce the number of rounds required to achieve a feasible plan.

Note that worker councils have no incentive to consistently underestimate their productive capability in the preparation of production proposals since this would involve a risk that their proposals are not approved and/or that they will not be assigned the inputs they want. If anything, there is a risk that workers will exaggerate their capabilities to win approval for their proposals during the planning process, which industry federations need to be concerned about. This risk is offset by the fact that the workplaces', i.e. their members', average consumption points in the end are based on actual SB/SC ratios from the work that is done and not on anticipated SB/SC ratios from the proposed work. However, if a worker council repeatedly fails to deliver in accordance with its approved production proposal, industry federations can revoke the worker council's membership in the industry federation. The worker council would then not be allowed to submit production proposals in next year's planning procedure.

In early iterations there is no problem if worker councils submit production proposals with SB/SC ratios less than one, or if consumer councils submit proposals their consumption points do not justify. As a matter of fact this behaviour generates useful information about where it is that worker and consumers would most like to see productive capabilities increased through investment and long-term development planning. As long as the IFB adjusts indicative prices up for whatever is in greatest excess demand and down for whatever is in greatest excess supply, and as long as councils approve what the ratios explained above indicate is efficient and fair, the participatory annual planning procedure will eventually reach a feasible plan that is also efficient and fair.

ADJUSTING A PLAN DURING THE YEAR

Circumstances and conditions will most likely change in the time between the preparation of a plan and the time for its implementation. Consumer preferences can change and unforeseen events will likely occur that affect producers circumstances as well. A large portion of the changes in consumers' preferences will presumably cancel out at the national level which make it possible to handle such changes within the framework of the production plan as it was approved. In cases where this is not possible, and when big unforeseen events occur that demand adjustments in production, necessary adjustments need to be negotiated by representatives from affected consumer and worker federations.

Some adjustments in the plan may need only small changes in the capacity utilisation in the production units in one industries, while other adjustments could be more far reaching and affect more workplaces and require a redistribution of resources between industries. Some adjustments may be accomplished via rationing of products without changing the prices while other adjustments may include price changes in order to fairly distribute the costs of the changes between various actors.

The important point at this moment is to note that it is quite possible to adjust a plan in light of changing circumstances, and that such adjustments in a participatory economy are made in democratic negotiations between representatives from both consumers and producers, possibly with help of the IFB.

SUMMARY

A Participatory Economy coordinates the elaborate division of labour between its many worker and consumer councils and federations via a particular kind of participatory planning procedure. It is a social process in which workers and consumers together, through their councils and federations, over a number of rounds of proposals, create a plan for the upcoming year's economic activities that is fair and efficient. Consumers and workers in different councils do not deliberate directly with each other, nor do they set their own prices. Instead, consumer and worker councils revise their own "self-activity proposals" in response to ever more accurate "signals" about opportunity and social costs and benefits generated by the planning procedure, in a context where they know other councils will only approve production proposals that are socially efficient and consumption proposals that are fair. Councils vote to approve or reject other council's proposals, but have no role in making changes in what other councils will do.

In the rest of the book we will discuss the implications that an implementation of the model's institutions *could have* on a future accounting model and its set of accounting principles. We will therefore also by necessity be more detailed in the descriptions of the institutions.

CHAPTER 2

THE ACTORS

In the previous chapter, which briefly summarised the participatory economics model, we outlined who the model's key actors and decision makers are: worker councils and their federations, consumer councils and their federations and an Iteration Facilitation Board (IFB). In this chapter we look a little closer at these actors, their roles and responsibilities.

CONSUMERS

In the annual planning procedure, individual households propose and adjust their planned consumption of goods and services for the upcoming year, based on the most recently announced prices set by the Iteration Facilitation Board. Consumers are restricted to how much they can request by their level of income. Income in a participatory economy is earned in four ways, through: **(i) performing socially valuable work** - consumption points are distributed to workers in the workplace based on their levels of effort or sacrifice, **(ii) compensation for damage caused by pollution** - citizens who are negatively affected by pollution receive compensation in the form of consumption points, **(iii) special needs requests within a consumer council or federation** - residents of the neighbourhood or members in a federation can decide to redistribute income between members based on need, or for other reasons as they see fit, and **(iv) national insurance schemes** – children too young to work, people who are retired, or severely disabled would be eligible to receive consumption points through national insurance schemes, which redistributes income on a national level.

Households may also borrow and save consumption points. A household's neighbourhood consumer council reviews and approves or rejects members' loan applications for greater consumption, and is responsible for ensuring that loans are repaid. Consumption points are saved for upcoming years when households consume less during a year than their consumption point allotment.

Members in a neighbourhood consumer council approve or reject the other members' consumption requests and elect representatives to higher federations of consumer councils. A fair proposal is one in which the social cost of providing the proposed consumption does not exceed a household's available consumption points. Proposals deemed to be unfair are generally rejected, and it is up to households to make revisions until its proposal is acceptable. This process takes place entirely within each neighbourhood consumer council.

Members of a neighbourhood consumer council also discuss and decide what neighbourhood public goods to request, such as playground facilities, sidewalks, leisure centres. All approved individual household proposals, plus approved local public goods and services comprise the neighbourhood consumer council proposal submitted during the national annual planning procedure. At each higher consumer federation level collective consumption is discussed and decided upon by recallable delegates from lower level member councils. Households are "charged" for their share of the social cost of providing all the different public goods they benefit from. Members at each level in the federation structure approve or reject the other members' requests.

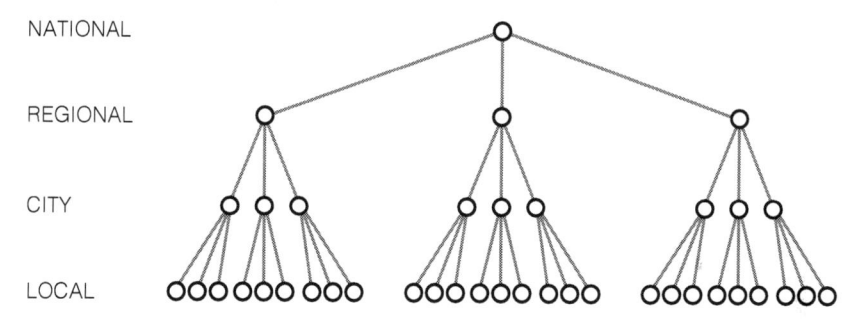

Figure 2.1. Federation structure

In addition to planning individual and collective consumption, consumers also participate in the participatory planning procedures for the pricing of pollution emissions from worker councils. In a participatory economy the polluters are charged for the damage that their pollution causes and the affected parties are compensated. Since the consumers affected by pollution do not always coincide with the geographical demarcations of the consumer councils and federations, a participatory economy needs to establish "Communities of Affected parties" (CAPs) - which gather together all those adversely affected by different pollutants into groups, regardless of which consumer council or federation they belong to. The compensation that consumers receive for the negative effects caused by pollution is added to the consumption points they earn in their workplaces and any consumption allowances they might have, and will thus affect the level of their possible consumption.

During an ongoing year, consumer federations also function as clearing houses where differences between members' planned and actual consumption can be offset against each other. Most differences between planned and actual consumption at the individual level can most likely be handled through internal redistribution within the consumer federations, but if the differences between total planned and actual consumption between all consumers do not cancel each other out, consumer federations act as a negotiating party with the industry federations in negotiations to adjust the current year's consumption and production plans.

These are the most important tasks and decisions faced by consumers in a participatory economy. The chronological and internal order of the decisions will largely follow from the detailed design of the planning procedures, but otherwise the consumers will design and organise their decision making routines entirely at their own discretion, and the routines in different councils and federations are likely to differ from each other.

WORKERS

During the annual planning procedure, individual worker councils prepare and adjust their production proposals for the upcoming year based on the most recent indicative prices from the IFB. A production proposal consists of quantities of the goods and services the worker council wants to produce, and the amounts of various inputs – natural resources, labour, capital goods, and intermediate goods – it wants permission to use to do so. A production proposal is basically an appeal to the rest of society: "If you give us permission to use and consume the resources specified in our proposal - resources which belong to all of society and therefore should benefit everyone - we promise to produce and deliver the goods and services specified in our proposal".

Every worker council is also responsible for organising tasks into jobs that are balanced for empowerment, and for distributing a fixed amount of consumption points among its members based on their efforts and sacrifices. As already explained, worker councils are free to design their own routines and procedures for these tasks and different workplaces are very likely to adopt different ways to measure effort and balance jobs.

Worker councils vote on whether or not to approve each other's proposals during the annual planning procedure by comparing the estimated social benefit of the goods and services to be produced with the estimated social costs of the resources expended in production - the SB/SC ratio. If this ratio is greater than one, the proposed use of resources is responsible, efficient, and all benefit by approving the proposal. If the ratio is less than one, the proposal is considered socially irresponsible and inefficient. In this case, there are presumably other worker councils who would use the resources more efficiently and responsibly. However, there may be exceptional circumstances when a worker council should be allowed to implement production proposal with an SB/SC ratio of less than 1. As already explained, there will need to be appeals procedures for special cases where "the numbers" may lie.

The SB/SC ratio in a workplace can also be used to set the cap on the average consumption points that a worker council can award its members. A cap is needed in order to prevent inflation in consumption points. If a workplace has a higher SB/SC ratio its members may be entitled to a correspondingly higher average income. The logic behind this way of capping average consumption points is that in theory the indicative prices of inputs already account for all reasons a workplace might have a higher SB/SC ratio *except* that its members have exerted greater effort. For example, if one workplace produced more output than another simply because it was using better machinery, this will presumably already be accounted for by a higher indicative price for the better machinery, so a workplace with better machinery will be charged more for using the better machinery. Alternatively, if people do not trust the indicative prices generated by the participatory planning procedure to fully level the playing field for worker councils, then the cap on average consumption points can be made the same for all workplaces.

All worker councils belong to an industry federation based on what they produce, and possibly a different federation based on their geographical location. Worker councils elect recallable representatives to these federations. Industry federations approve or reject applications for membership in the federation based on assessments of the applicant worker councils' reliability, i.e. is there reason to believe they can actually do what they propose. Membership in an industry federation means that the worker council can participate in the annual planning procedure and submit production proposals for gaining access to productive resources. Industry federations may also organise shared support functions funded by all member councils. And finally, industry federations act as negotiating parties if a plan needs to be adjusted during a year;

for example, due to large changes in consumers' preferences or other unforeseen events.

FEDERATIONS AND LONG TERM PLANNING

Besides annual planning, a participatory economy needs to engage in investment planning to increase and adjust stocks of capital goods needed for production, and also in long-term development planning to respond sensibly to anticipated changes in the international division of labour and technologies, and to "plan" desirable changes in the supplies of different kinds of labour and natural resources to be available for annual planning in the future. For example, right now a participatory economy would decide how much to reduce carbon emissions by 2050 during its long run planning process, and this decision would become an important constraint on its five year investment plans as well as its annual plans between now and then. However, investment and particularly long term development planning face important difficulties that annual planning does not. The amount of uncertainty regarding technologies, preferences, international, and environmental conditions escalates rapidly the further forward in time we go. Most importantly this means that estimating what future opportunity and social costs will be becomes problematic because they will depend on what development and investment plans are adopted, which introduces a troublesome circular dependency that makes today's opportunity and social costs unreliable as a basis for decisions about longer-term investments.

The goals and fundamental values of a participatory economy, such as self-management and economic justice, of course also apply to longer-term planning as well. However, it is reasonable to assume that the preparation of long-term plans will have to allow for consumer and worker council representatives in higher level federations to play a bigger part at the expense of individual consumer and worker councils, and that researchers in R&D units with expertise in various areas will play a more prominent role in explaining and describing possible alternative development scenarios. Furthermore, long-term planning will require a greater element of discussions between representatives of consumers, workers and experts to formulate alternative plans, and consist less of "self-activity" proposals from individual consumer and worker councils.

The federations made up of consumer and producer representatives, with the support of experts and researchers, need to make decisions about how they want the long-term development and the direction of investment, production and consumption in the economy to look like. This is called long-term **development planning**. Issues that the development planning needs to deal with may include questions about society's energy supply, introduction of new production technologies, organisation of infrastructure, and so on. Should energy supply be transformed from fossil fuels to renewables, and if so, how fast and in what order? How fast and in what manner should transport by car be replaced by public transport? How do we want the agricultural sector's use of chemical fertilisers to be developed? Do we want to invest in the development of any particular industry sector and does this have an impact on the trade exchanges that we want to have with external economies; and what products do we want to import and export? Should we prioritise research and development in any specific area?

In light of the long-term development plan the next task is to create a more concrete **investment plan**, which basically determines the playing field for the upcoming years with regard to changes in stocks of produced capital goods and infrastructure. An important issue the investment plan must settle is how society's total production should be distributed between production of investment goods and consumption goods. Investment means that society "sacrifices" consumption in the short term in order to expand its productive capacity in the long term. Once the decision about the distribution between investment and consumption has been made, investment planning is about deciding which capital good stocks should be increased more or less, and which industries should increase their productive capacity in the next years and by how much; what specific investments in various categories of capital, R&D and education initiatives do we want. When the annual planning process starts all these investment decisions have been made, which means that not only are the supplies of various categories of capital, natural resources, and labour known and set, the amount of each capital good we must make during the year is set as well. The annual planning procedure is then about deciding which worker councils will get access to which resources.

In order to sensibly assess whether an investment or a long term project is acceptable from a social perspective, decision makers need an estimate of the "social return of investment" (SROI) for different investment projects, i.e. the social benefits that investments are expected to generate in relation to the social costs they require over time. The longer-term the investments the more difficult it is to estimate the SROI and the greater uncertainty and greater element of speculation in assessments.

THE ITERATION FACILITATION BOARD

The Iteration Facilitation Board (IFB) is an actor with limited decision-making power, except of course in matters relating to its own internal working conditions. It is funded collectively and acts based on society's instructions. The IFB's main task is to update the indicative prices for all categories of capital, resources, labour, goods and services, and for emissions of different categories of pollutants before each new iteration during the annual planning procedure and also during the year in cases when the annual plan must be updated. The updates of the indicative prices are based on the excess supply or demand that emerges through the actors proposals for production and consumption. By analysing historical data and statistics the IFB can estimate how actors will respond to price changes for different products, i.e. different products price elasticity.

The IFB's responsibilities may also include to enable and facilitate the flow of information generally in the economy, which could include developing and providing systems for the collection, dissemination and evaluation of information, as well as calculation and allocation of consumption points to worker councils. Exactly what should be included in the IFB's assignment, how extensive or limited it should be, and whether there should be checks and limits on how long a worker can serve on the IFB because its work tasks are more empowering than average, is of course something that citizens in a future participatory economy need to decide for themselves.

CHAPTER 3

THE ACCOUNTING SYSTEM

The challenge for a participatory economy is to distribute power and influence over decisions to economic agents in a way that promotes efficiency, while achieving self-management and justice. Some economic decisions affect all members in an economy, others affect only certain groups, while most decisions affect different parties to different extents. The participatory planning procedures are designed precisely to address these challenges. Therefore, the main task for an accounting system in a participatory economy, is to provide the information that is necessary for the implementation of the participatory planning procedures. In this chapter we want to give a picture of how such an accounting system could work.

THE GENERAL PURPOSE OF ACCOUNTING IN A PARTICIPATORY ECONOMY

The main objectives for an accounting system for a participatory economy should be to enable and promote the:

1. Planning of future economic activity in three separate planning procedures with different time horizons - long-term development planning, investment planning and annual planning.

2. Recording of economic transactions during the current year.

3. Continuous monitoring and evaluation of outcomes in relation to plan for various activities, and possible adjustments of the current annual plan and other future plans.

In order to achieve these goals the design of the accounting system must permit economic actors to correctly estimate, record and evaluate: (i) the opportunity costs of using various categories of labour, natural resources such as agricultural land and forests, and produced capital such as factory buildings and equipment, (ii) the social costs of producing and consuming various goods and services, (iii) the damage, or social cost of emissions of different pollutants, and (iv) as best possible the social rate of return on investment in expanding different aspects of the productive capacity operative over many years.

In this context there are a number of issues of technical and practical nature to consider that are not primarily about the rules and design of the participatory planning procedure. A crucial practical and technical issue is how all the different varieties of goods, services, capital, resources and emissions of polluting substances should be defined, categorised and quantified so that; a) consumers and workers can relate to them in an accurate and efficient way, b) their prices will reflect the opportunity costs of productive resources and the social costs of goods and services, c) a viable, fair and efficient annual plan will emerge in the annual planning procedure and d) an efficient monitoring of the annual plan is facilitated. In order to achieve this, different types of goods, services and resources will each require a different basis for categorisation.

In the following chapters, we will focus on these practical and technical issues, but the first step on our way to developing an accounting model for a participatory economy is to identify the main accounting entities and their transactions, which together form the accounting system's structure or "skeleton". Only then can we move on to focus on how the entities different economic activities can be defined and categorised so that the overall goals of the accounting model *and* of the participatory economics model as a whole - economic democracy and justice, solidarity, diversity, ecological sustainability and efficiency - can be achieved.

ACCOUNTING ENTITIES AND TRANSACTIONS

In our proposed accounting system we identify five main categories of accounting entities whose economic activities and transactions are recorded and monitored in order to facilitate effective and fair decisions, and two "reconciliation entities" which are used to create units for consumption rights (consumption points).

Primary accounting entities:

1. Consumers, consumer councils and federations
2. Worker councils
3. Industry Federations' stocks of manufactured productive capital
4. Industry Federations' stocks of natural capital
5. Society's Investment Fund

Reconciliation entities:

1. Reconciliation entity for work compensation
2. Reconciliation entity for compensation for damage caused by pollution

In this section we describe each of the five categories of accounting entities and the economic transactions that need to be recorded for each entity, and the information for facilitating decision making which thus emerges. The two reconciliation entities are described in the next section. The purpose of the reconciliation entities is to facilitate the transformation of worker councils' costs for labour and emissions of pollutants into consumption rights, or consumption points, to be distributed to workers and affected parties as compensation or income.

The economic transactions identified below can in principle refer to both planned activities and actual performed activities, depending on whether it is the planning of future activities or the recording of actual transactions for the year in focus. Every accounting entity and its accounts exist in two versions: one for planning purposes and one for the recording of actual transactions. The actual outcome is continually compared to the plan as the year progresses. Actual transactions during a year are normally recorded at a more detailed level compared to planned transactions which means that there are more sub-accounts in the actual outcome version compared to the annual planning version. At the end of this chapter there is a flow chart that provides an overview of the economic transactions between different accounting entities in a participatory economy.

The descriptions of the accounting and monitoring of economic transactions in this book are in most cases based on an overall socio-economic perspective and can partly be compared to what today is called external financial accounting as opposed to internal management cost accounting. Individual worker councils in a participatory economy may very well develop their own internal accounting routines in order to create more detailed decision support for internal decisions.

Money and Prices

A participatory economy will most likely not use money in the sense of notes and coins in order to facilitate, register and monitor the exchange of goods and services and other financial transactions. A participatory economy will likely instead use a form of more or less immaterial *"currency units"* which are recorded in, and circulates between, different actors' accounts. When we in the following refer to consumption points, income, social costs, social benefits etc., it is basically such currency units we're referring to. Transfers of currency units between accounts due to economic transactions can in most cases easily be managed electronically using technology that exists already today, such as the use of debit and credit cards, online payment processing, and so on, possibly supplemented by vouchers in the unlikely event that it would be needed, where the coupons would reflect the decisions in the annual planning regarding consumption and production by individuals and councils.

In a participatory economy, as with other types of economic systems, all inputs and outputs have prices. *Prices* in a participatory economy are defined as estimates of opportunity costs for using scarce productive resources, and estimates of the social costs (and benefits) of producing intermediate, final goods and services. Whenever we use natural capital (land, forests, water, etc.), labour (nurses, plumbers, accountants, etc.) or manufactured capital (factories, machines, etc.) there is always an *'opportunity cost'* because there is a loss of potential gain from other alternative uses. With intermediate goods (e.g. aluminium, leather, etc.) or final goods (shoes, libraries, bicycles, etc.), since producing them consumes scarce inputs and requires us to forego leisure, there are *'social costs'* of producing them.

While prices will always be imperfect estimates, and therefore should always be considered as 'indicative', they are useful as a means to help consumers and workers in making decisions regarding the use of different scarce productive resources, and to assess the social costs of producing different goods and services. Prices in a participatory economy are generated in a very different way than in a market system. In a participatory economy, they are not set by individual buyers and sellers in competitive bargaining situations. Instead prices are generated through a democratic social planning procedure that reveals the benefits and costs of using goods and services to all those that are affected.

Throughout this book, we want to stress that whenever we use the term prices, they are always meant as estimates of opportunity and social costs (and benefits) and that these estimates emerge from a participatory, social planning procedure – not from the grinding of the laws of supply and demand as in market systems.

Performing accounting tasks

Finally, before we move on to looking more closely at the details of our accounting system, we want to briefly say something about the organisation of the actual work of recording and analysing economic transactions in a participatory economy, and how it is likely to differ from how today's capitalist companies organise their finance departments. In multinational corporations, joint administration or accounting centres are often responsible for accounting, bookkeeping and financial analyses where senior officials and auditors control and, wherever possible, restrict access to and dissemination of financial information, both internally and externally. In a participatory economy, in contrast, all forms of accounting information is completely transparent and available to anyone and everyone who is interested.

The responsibility for preparing and submitting production and consumption proposals in the annual planning lies with the individual worker councils and consumer neighbourhood councils. Specially established shared industry support units without any decision-making power, or alternatively the IFB, could in this context be assigned to assist individual worker councils during the annual planning if such needs are identified. The responsibility for recording economic transactions during a year, and for analysing and managing deviations between a year's actual results and the annual plan could also be assigned to shared support units, or to the IFB, even if the individual worker councils also establish their own accounting committees or units, with the task of managing, interpreting and analysing accounting information. The exact division of responsibility between a worker council's own accounting department and an industry's shared support unit, with regard to accounting tasks, such as recording, analysing and monitoring economic transactions, is obviously a matter for a future participatory economy and the worker councils and their industry federations to decide.

CONSUMERS AND THEIR FEDERATIONS

The first obvious group of primary accounting entities to monitor in a participatory economy is the *consumers and their councils and federations*. Every consumer council and federation is a separate entity with its own account. Every individual consumer also has their own separate account[12]. Incoming consumption points from worker councils as compensation for work performed and from CAPs as compensation for damage from pollution are credited to the individual consumer's account. All costs for consumed goods and services, both individually and collectively consumed, are distributed and charged to the consumers' accounts through a number of cost centres, every one of which belonging to a council or a federation. We describe the cost centres, the internal relations between various consumer accounting entities, and the accounting of transfers of consumption points and costs of consumed goods and services in more detail in the next chapter.

CONSUMPTION, DEBT AND SAVINGS	
Dr	Cr
2) Expenses & loans: Consumed goods / services per category:	1) Income & savings: consumption points:
a) individual consumption	a) from work
b) collective consumption	b) through CAPs - compensation for pollution
c) collective investment	c) redistributions (Dr/Cr)
3) Net debt from earlier years	4) Net savings from earlier years

Figure 3.1. Accounts: Consumers, Consumer Councils and Federations[13]

When a consumer receives consumption points, the consumer's account is credited with the amount and with an identification of the source. Consumers receive consumption points from two external sources, (1) as compensation for work performed from the worker council in which

---

12 The accounts of individual consumers in a participatory economy can to some degree be compared to transaction accounts or similar in our banks to which debit or credit cards can be attached.

13 Since there is no need to closely identify and monitor consumers assets and liabilities in a participatory economy but only their compensation in the form of consumption points (including internal transfers between consumers and compensations from CAP) and their use of consumption points via consumption we use an "impure" form of single entry accounting to follow up and register *consumers* transactions in our accounting model. Of course it would be quite possible to use double entry accounting instead.

they work, and (2) as members of CAPs, through which consumption points are obtained as compensation for the damage caused by emissions of pollutants. A neighbourhood council can decide to reallocate consumption points between individual members' accounts based on differences in need. There will presumably also be a national insurance system for redistribution of income to children, the retired and those too disabled to work. A portion of a household's consumption points will be used for collective consumption at different federation levels. Collectively financed consumption means that consumption points are transferred from the individual consumer's or household's account - which is debited - to the account of the council or federation that requested the collective consumption, which is credited.

When an individual consumer picks up a good at the distribution centre or uses a service, her account will be charged with the social cost of the actual individual product or service. Costs for *collectively financed* consumption are charged to the account of the relevant consumer council or federation via cost centres, which represent the workplaces that provide the good or service. We will return to how collective consumption and associated costs are decided, recorded, allocated and monitored in the next chapter.

Both individual households and councils can save consumption points for future years by consuming less than their income allows for one year in order to allow for greater consumption in upcoming years, or borrow consumption points by consuming more than their income allows for one year and repaying by consuming less in future years. The latter requires approval from the other members. Savings and loans are visible as credit and debit net balances on each account and are carried forward to coming years, with the approval of neighbourhood councils in the case of loans.

Members in a neighbourhood consumer council, and in a federation, can assess the other respective members' consumption proposals by verifying that the available consumption points including points from work, CAPs, transfers, savings and approved loans, are equivalent to the total charges for individual and collective consumption. This way, individual consumers, consumer councils and federations can easily assess whether their own and other members' consumption is fair. Consumption is fair if total earned and assigned consumption points in an account are on par with or in excess of the total charged social cost of individual and collective consumption. Consumption is unfair if the total number of consumption points is less than the social cost of the consumption.

WORKER COUNCILS

The second obvious group of accounting entities to pay attention to in a participatory economy is **the worker councils**. In a participatory economy there are no privately owned companies and therefore no accounting of "Equity" corresponding to private owners' claims on company net assets. Nor are there any private credit institutions which fund acquisitions of productive capital resources through loans that are recorded as external liabilities to financial institutions or banks in the books of corporations. Productive capital resources are not even owned by the worker councils, but belong to all citizens in the society, and during the annual planning procedure various worker councils apply for the right to use different productive resources in exchange for a promise to provide goods and services.

Deliveries of goods and services, and procurement of materials etc. are credited or charged to the worker councils immediately upon delivery without a need to record payables and receivables. However, credit entries for deliveries can be made contingent on approval by the receiving party. Furthermore, worker councils do sometimes make use of short-term "credit" in the sense that the charge for acquired and utilised resources often appear before the credit entries for deliveries of produced goods and services. In addition, certain large charges may need to be spread over several years - accrued - for accounting purposes in order to accurately reflect a worker council's utilisation of acquired resources. After a completed year, there will be no dividends of profits paid out to private owners. Any surplus or deficit that worker councils produce will be transferred to "society", and not to individuals.

Every individual worker council represents an accounting entity, the economic transactions of which are recorded and monitored[14]. Available funds, the accrual of certain large debit entries, and the balance to society and industry federations are recorded and managed with the help of a number of accounts for short term social assets (account category 1 and

---

14 Accounting of economic transactions on the producer side is done by using conventional double entry accounting.

SHORT TERM SOCIAL ASSETS	
Dr	Cr
1.a) Available funds	2.) Society & industry federations - balance
1.b) Accruals - intermediate goods	
1.c) Inventory	

SOCIAL BENEFITS AND COSTS	
Dr	Cr
4.) Social costs:	3.) Social benefits:
a) input goods/services	a) delivered goods/services
b) emissions of pollutants	
c) use of produced capital - user rights	
d) use of natural capital - user rights	
e) use of labour - user rights	
f) accrual accounts - inventory	
g) accrual accounts – other items	
5.) Period closing (Dr/Cr)	

DISTRIBUTION OF CONSUMPTION POINTS	
Dr	Cr
Internally allocated consumption points	*Received consumption points to allocate*

Figure 3.2 Worker councils: Economic statements

2 in figure 3.2), which to some degree can be thought of as the equivalent to a company's balance accounts in a capitalist economy. Credit entries for deliveries of produced goods and services, and debit entries for the acquisition of inputs, usage of categories of labour and productive capital are recorded in accounts for social benefits and social costs (account category 3 and 4 in figure 3.2), the equivalent to revenue and cost accounts in a capitalist company, if you will. Individual worker councils' economic statements may for some decisions and analyses be consolidated by industry i.e. summarised at the industry level.

Every worker council also has to distribute consumption points to its members based on their effort and sacrifice in the workplace. The council is allocated a total sum of consumption points that it can distribute among its members, which are recorded in credit in an internal reconciliation account for the distribution of consumption points. How the size of this sum is determined is described in *chapter 5: Work and Production*. When the points are then distributed to the members, the reconciliation account is debited. All consumption points that are assigned to a worker council are distributed to its members. Entries in the internal reconciliation account for consumption points do not affect a council's SB/SC ratio, but merely facilitate the monitoring of the allocation of consumption points to its members.

Below and in the rest of the book we will propose specific accounting entries for economic transactions that the accounting entities in our accounting model perform. The numbers and account names in the suggested entries refer to account categories in the economic statements of "Social assets" and "Social benefits and costs".

Delivering a good or service

When a worker council delivers its produced goods to the distribution centres in a neighbourhood council or to another worker council, or when it performs a service, the relevant sub-account identifying the correct category of good or service in account category *3.a) Social benefits* is credited with an amount calculated as the *delivered quantity* multiplied with the *price* that was settled in the annual planning procedure. Account *1.a.) Available funds* is debited with the same amount.

| OUTBOUND DELIVERY OF PRODUCED GOODS / SERVICES ||
Dr	Cr
1.a) Available funds	3.a) Social benefits delivered goods/services

Receiving a good or using a service

When a council receives goods or uses services from other worker councils, the relevant sub-account identifying the correct category of good or service in account category *4.a) Social costs* is charged with an amount calculated in the same way as outbound deliveries i.e. quantity times the price from the annual planning procedure. Account *1.a.) Available funds* is credited with the same amount.

RECEIVING A GOOD OR USING A SERVICE	
Dr	Cr
4.a) Social costs: input goods/services	1.a) Available funds

Using productive resources and emitting pollutants

Emissions of pollutants and the use of different categories of manufactured and natural capital, and labour are handled in exactly the same way. Relevant sub-accounts in account category *4.) Social costs* are charged with costs for damages caused by different pollutants and with user right fees for different categories of capital and labour, with an amount calculated in the same way as for any other use of goods, services and resources. Account *1.a) Available funds* is credited.

THE EMISSION OF POLLUTANTS AND USE OF PRODUCTIVE RESOURCES	
Dr	Cr
4.b-e) Social costs …	1.a) Available funds

Accruals

Some resources that are not classified as capital may still have a lifespan of several years, and other inputs and produced goods may need to be stored for some time before being used or delivered. These facts suggest that worker councils need to be able to allocate certain costs over several years in order for the accounting information for individual years to be true and accurate.[15] At the same time, such possibilities for cost accruals open up opportunities for accounting manipulations that industry federations need to be aware of and control.[16] In Appendix 2 we describe how accruals of costs for inputs and inventory could be handled.

---

15   The accounting of cost accruals in our participatory economy accounting model is in principle the same as in today's capitalist economy.

16   The industry federations could for instance control and limit the worker councils' possibilities to propose large increases of inventory in individual years.

Provisions for shared federation resources

A worker council may, based on decisions by industry federations, earmark part of its balance to society, for shared research projects and other shared resources and support units within the industry federation. Such provisions are charged to the worker council as a cost and credited to the relevant sub-account in account 2.) *Society and industry federations – balance.*

Period closing

The difference between the value of a worker council's credited social benefit and charged social costs will in the end accrue to society and affect society's capacity for investments and shared resources. After a completed year (or more often) the difference between credited social benefit and charged social costs is transferred to account 2.) *Society and industry federations - balance* by a year-end closing entry...[17]

PERIOD CLOSING - SURPLUS	
Dr	Cr
5.) Period closing	2.) Society and industry federations - balance

PERIOD CLOSING - DEFICIT	
Dr	Cr
2) Society and industry federations - balance	5.) Period closing

...after which available funds are transferred to society's investment fund, which reduces the worker council's balance to society and industry federation.[18]

TRANSFER OF AVAILABLE FUNDS TO SOCIETY	
Dr	Cr
2) Society and industry federations - balance	1.a) Available funds

---

17 The equivalent to a year end closing transaction in a capitalist company where the ending year's profit or loss is transferred to Equity.

18 The equivalent, if you will, to dividends in a capitalist company.

Based on the information that emerges from the compilation of economic transactions, a worker council can quickly and easily assess whether their own and other councils' planned or real production is efficient and socially responsible. A worker councils production is efficient from the perspective of society if its SB/SC ratio exceeds 1, i.e. if the total credited social benefit for all their deliveries of goods and services (account category 3) *is greater* than the total sum of charged social costs for the production of the same goods and services (account category 4). A worker council's production is inefficient if the SB/SC ratio is *less* than 1, i.e. if their total credited social benefit is less than the total sum of charged social costs for the production.

The two groups of accounting entities that we have identified so far – consumers and their councils and federations, and worker councils - are the primary actors in a participatory economy, which plan and execute economic activities during the annual planning procedure and during the year. The accounting of economic transactions as described above allow these actors to decide whether their own and others' activities - both planned and realised - are fair, efficient and responsible.

THE INDUSTRY FEDERATIONS' STOCKS OF MANUFACTURED CAPITAL

The remaining three categories of accounting entities do not correspond to *acting* worker councils or consumer councils. They can rather be seen as a form of *passive* entities whose main purpose is to coordinate and structure economic information in a way that, as far as possible, facilitate decisions concerning the direction of society's long-term development, various industries' productive capacity, concrete investments, training and education, research and development, infrastructure, shared resources, trade etc.[19] In this context, the focus is on social return on investment for investments or projects. First we look at the **industry federations' stocks of manufactured productive capital**.

As already noted, in a participatory economy it is not privately owned companies, capitalists or creditors who own and control the productive

---

19 The descriptions of the passive accounting entities in the next three sections of the chapter may be perceived as difficult to follow without previous knowledge of accounting theory.

assets (e.g. buildings, machines, tools, etc.), or decide which investments society should make, or who will get to use them. In the investment planning, which will be described later, representatives from federations of worker councils and consumer councils decide how the productive capacity of different industries will be developed in the years to come and thus how their stock of productive manufactured capital will be composed. The distribution of *user rights* to productive capital assets among individual worker councils, however, is determined during the annual planning procedure.

Every industry federation with its associated stock of manufactured productive capital assets constitutes a separate accounting entity for which transactions are planned, recorded and monitored. Federations may also be split up into smaller administrative units based on geographical divisions which can be consolidated into ever larger sectors or geographical areas for analysis and monitoring. Industry federations do not "own" assets but they have access to them in accordance to the latest investment plan for further distribution to individual worker councils in the annual planning.

SOCIAL ASSETS	
Dr	Cr
1.a) Available funds	2.) Society - balance
1.ba) Acquisition cost per category of capital	
1.bb) Accumulated depreciation per category of capital (Cr)	
SOCIAL BENEFITS AND COSTS	
Dr	Cr
4.a) Annual depreciation of capital (per category of capital)	3.) Incoming user right fees (per category of capital)
4.b) Maintenance costs etc. per category of capital)	
5.) Period closing (Dr/Cr)	

Figure 3.3. Industry Federations stocks of produced productive capital: Economic statement.

Available funds, acquisition costs of assets, accumulated depreciation, and balance to society are recorded in a number of accounts for social assets (categories 1 and 2 in figure 3.3.). Credit entries for incoming user right fees from worker councils that use the capital assets, annual depreciation of the assets' acquisition costs, and costs for maintenance that the industry federations should bear are recorded and monitored via a number of accounts under "Social benefits and costs" (category 3 and 4 in figure 3.3.). Any surplus or deficit is transferred to society.

Expansion of capital stock

When the stock of capital assets for an industry federation is expanded in accordance with the approved investment plan, i.e. when new productive capital is added to existing assets or when existing capital is transferred from another industry, the relevant sub-account for the correct capital category in account category *1.ba) Acquisition costs* of productive capital is charged with the acquisition cost, with a corresponding credit entry in account *2.) Society - balance.*

EXPANDING THE STOCK OF PRODUCTIVE CAPITAL - INVESTMENT	
Dr	Cr
1.ba) Acquisition cost per category of capital	2.) Society - balance

Depreciations

Annual depreciations are recorded during a capital asset's economic life. The annual depreciation amount should reflect the yearly consumption of the asset. The relevant sub-account in account category *1.bb) Accumulated depreciation* is credited with an amount that is calculated based on current depreciation policies, and thus reduces the assets net value. A corresponding sub-account in the account category *4.a) Annual depreciation* is charged with the same amount.

DEPRECIATION OF CAPITAL ASSETS	
Dr	Cr
4.a) Annual depreciation of capital per category	1.bb) Accumulated depreciation per category of capital

Use of capital asset

When a member council belonging to an industry federation is given access to existing productive capital assets, the *worker council* is charged a fee for the right to use the assets, whose size is determined in the annual planning procedure.[20] At the same time, the industry federation's account *1.a) Available funds* is debited, and the relevant sub-account for capital category in account category *3.) Incoming user right fees* is credited with the user right fee.

MEMBER COUNCIL IS GRANTED ACCESS TO A CAPITAL ASSET	
Dr	Cr
1.a) Available funds	3.) Incoming user right fees per category of capital

Maintenance

Costs for maintenance work and any other costs[21] required to ensure the functionality of productive capital assets *may* be handled by the industry federation and financed by the user right fees that worker councils pay. In this case, it is the industry federation's sub-account for the relevant category of capital in account category *4.b) Maintenance costs etc.* that is charged when such work is performed, and account *1.a.) Available funds* is credited.

MAINTENANCE OF CAPITAL ASSETS	
Dr	Cr
4.b) Maintenance costs etc. per category of capital	1.a) Available funds

Period closing

Incoming user right fees after the reduction of charges for maintenance costs will in the end accrue to society and affect society's capacity for

---

20 In *Chapter 5: Work and production* we examine closer how user rights for productive resources are priced and how capital assets can be categorised.

21 Certain capital assets and facilities, mainly for service production, may be provided by the consumer councils. Industry federations that are gives access to such assets could be charged with a portion of the costs for providing and maintaining these facilities that the consumer council incur.

investments. After a completed year (or more often) any difference between credit entries and charges in account categories 3.) and 4.) is transferred to account 2.) Society – balance, by a year-end closing entry...

PERIOD CLOSING - SURPLUS	
Dr	Cr
5.) Period closing	2.) Society - balance
PERIOD CLOSING - DEFICIT	
Dr	Cr
2.) Society - balance	5.) Period closing

...after which available funds are transferred to society's investment fund, which reduces the balance owed to society. Note that funds available for transferring is only affected by incoming user right fees and charged maintenance costs, *and not by the depreciation* of productive capital.

TRANSFER OF AVAILABLE FUNDS TO SOCIETY	
Dr	Cr
2) Society - balance	1.a) Available funds

By selecting different intervals of sub-accounts in account categories *3) and 4)* an industry federation can identify incoming user right fees for all the industry's capital assets, or capital assets used in a specific production technology, or for a specific category of capital, and compare them with the period's consumption of the capital assets in question i.e. the depreciation costs, with the addition of maintenance costs. If the incoming user right fees exceed the consumption of capital assets plus maintenance costs, it is an indication that the supply of such capital categories perhaps should be increased in coming years. If the incoming user right fees do not cover the consumption of capital assets and maintenance costs, it is an indication that the supply of such capital categories perhaps should be reduced in coming years.

THE INDUSTRY FEDERATIONS' STOCKS OF NATURAL CAPITAL

The next category of accounting entities is the **industry federations' stocks of natural capital** that they have access to in accordance to the long-term development planning and investment planning.[22] It may be natural productive resources such as agricultural land, forests, fishing waters etc. Each industry federation with their associated stock of natural capital constitutes a separate entity for which transactions are recorded and monitored. Also in this case the industry federations may be divided into smaller administrative units based on geographical boundaries and consolidated by industry or increasingly larger geographical areas for analysis and monitoring.

Available funds and balances to society are recorded in a number of accounts for social assets (categories 1 and 2 in figure 3.4). Credit entries for incoming user right fees from worker councils belonging to the federations, which use natural capital assets, are recorded on accounts under "Social benefits" (category 3 in figure 3.4). Any surplus is transferred to society.

SOCIAL ASSETS	
Dr	Cr
1.a) Available funds	2.) Society - balance
1.b) Identified natural resources	
SOCIAL BENEFITS	
Dr	Cr
4.) Period closing	3.) Incoming user right fees per category of capital

Figure 3.4. Industry Federations stock of natural capital: Economic statements

Natural capital are different categories of natural resources, which by definition cannot be manufactured but are provided by nature, and therefore has no manufacturing or acquisition cost. Different industries identify

---

[22] There could be just one common category of accounting entities for both manufactured and natural capital. However, for clarity, in this presentation we work with two separate categories of accounting entities for capital.

and are "granted access" to natural resources in the investment planning when the development of different industries' capacity is planned.

Use of natural resource

When a *worker council* is granted access to a natural capital asset, it is charged with a user right fee, the size of which is determined in the annual planning procedure. Incoming fees from worker councils for user rights are debited the industry federation account *1.a) Available funds*, and credited the relevant sub-account for the correct category of natural capital in account category *3) Incoming user right fees*.

MEMBER COUNCIL IS GRANTED ACCESS TO A NATURAL RESOURCE	
Dr	Cr
1.a) Available funds	3.) Incoming user right fees per category of capital

Period closing

Incoming user right fees will in the end accrue to society and affect society's capacity for investments. After a completed year the balance in account category *3.) Incoming user right fees* is transferred to account *2.) Society - balance* by a period closing entry ...

PERIOD CLOSING	
Dr	Cr
4.) Period closing	2.) Society - balance

...after which available funds are transferred to society's investment fund, which reduces the balance owed to society.

TRANSFER OF AVAILABLE FUNDS TO SOCIETY	
Dr	Cr
2) Society - balance	1.a) Available funds

Based on the information from the accounting system the industry federations can follow social return for different categories of natural capital and use this information as input for decisions about the future use of different categories of natural capital assets. When making such decisions society needs to consider other aspects as well, that are much harder to assess, such as the effects on the environment and the interests of future generations.

SOCIETY'S INVESTMENT FUND

The last of the five categories of accounting entities could be called *society's fund for investments and shared resources* or for brevity **Society's Investment Fund**. This is where the incoming funds, which the members of the worker councils control as producers, and the investments and fund allocations made based on the agreed on investment plan are recorded. Society's Investment Fund may be organised in a national unit, and several regional and industry units reflecting different regions' and federations' influence over fund allocation during the investment planning.

Together with the recording and monitoring of productive capital in the federations, the inflow of funds to "Society's investment fund" provide information for the calculation of social return on investment (SROI) for different *historical and previously implemented* investments and projects.

"Society's investment fund", see figure 3.5, has one account for available funds (account category 1), and one account for balanced investment funds (account category 2) in which not utilised, or over utilised, investment funds from previous years may be recorded. A difference between credit entries for inflow of settlements from other accounting entities (account category 3) and investments, including funds for shared resources, (account category 4) in an individual year may be cleared against the account for *balanced investment funds* at period end. If the annual inflow of funds exceed total investments, *balanced investment funds* is increased (Cr), and if the total investments exceed the inflow of funds from other entities, *balanced investment funds* is reduced (Dt). *Alternatively, the economy may decide to write off all such not utilised, or over utilised funds at the end of a year and start every new year fresh.*[23]

---

23 If recorded, accumulated balanced, not used, investment funds would appear as a credit balance in the account for *balanced investment funds* and would be matched by a debit balance in the account for *available funds*. Balanced overused investment funds would in principle be a debt to the future, and would appear as a debit balance on the account for *balanced investment funds* and would be matched by a negative balance in the account for *available funds*.

Inflow of funds from other accounting entities are specified by industry in sub-accounts under account category 3.) *Settlements from other entities*, and annual investment projects are specified in sub-accounts in account category 4.) *Investments and shared resources*.

FUNDS - BALANCES	
Dr	Cr
1.) Available funds	2.) Balanced investment funds
SETTLEMENTS FROM OTHER ENTITIES AND INVESTMENTS	
Dr	Cr
4.) Investments and shared resources - Industry federations	3.) Settlements from other entities
a) Productive capital	a) Worker councils
b) Support units	b) Manufactured capital - Industry federations
c) Research and development	c) Natural capital - Industry federations
d) Training and education	5.b) Period end - overspent funds
e) Other investments	
5.a) Period end - unused funds	

Figure 3.5. Society's Investment Fund: Economic statement of funds and investments

The economy also needs to follow up and decide on issues regarding trade with other economies, the balance between export and import, import restrictions, duties and other potential transactions with external economies. We will return to a discussion of these issues and their accounting technicalities in a separate section in *chapter 6: Long-term Planning*.

Inflow of funds

The inflow of funds to be used for investments and shared resources comes from three sources:

1. Funds from worker councils - account category *3.a) Settlements: Worker councils*

2. Funds from the use of manufactured capital - account category *3.b) Settlements: Manufactured capital by industry federation*
3. Funds from the use of natural capital - account category *3.c) Settlements: Natural capital by industry federation.*

Settlements are identified by industry. The relevant sub-account for industry in account category *3.) Settlements* is credited. Account *1.) Available funds* is debited.

INFLOW OF FUNDS - SETTLEMENTS	
Dr	Cr
1.) Available funds	3.a-c) Settlements

Worker councils and federations may earmark some of their settlement payments for industry specific projects and activities, such as R&D and industry support units. Such funds are controlled and allocated by the relevant industry federation.

Overall and over time, the total inflow of funds in our model reflects society's capacity for investments. At the same time, the inflow of funds can be affected by the planned level of investments. The more of society's resources that are used for investments and for the production of capital goods, the fewer resources can be used for the production of consumer goods. An increase in planned investments (all else being equal) signals and reflects an expectation that worker councils and the stocks of capital assets will increase their surpluses (which in the end will accrue to the investment fund). A surplus that is invested means that society saves resources for future consumption. In individual years, the capacity for investments can be affected by consumers' net savings, which will increase the capacity for investments, or consumers' net borrowing, which will decrease the capacity for investments. However, in our model society's savings and thus the capacity for investments are first and foremost indicated by the surpluses in the worker councils and the federations' stocks of capital assets.

Society's investments

Society's various types of investments and projects have different characteristics with different specific requirements for decision making information. Some investments, in the sense of large expenditures that generate benefits to society many years into the future, primarily affect citizens in their capacity as consumers, and should therefore, according to the self-management principle, be considered as a kind of collective *consumption* to be managed by the consumer federations. Such investments are described in the next chapter. Here we focus on investments that are funded by society's investment fund as described above and that are decided and agreed on in the investment planning.

Society has to decide on the long term development of the productive capacity for different industries and it needs in this context to get an idea of alternative projects' expected social return on investment, and weigh various arguments, opinions and alternatives against each other. A participatory economy prepares investment and development programs with different time aspects. Investment programs should include relatively detailed descriptions of the coming years' investments.

It is obviously difficult to predict all possible future effects of an investment, but some guidance can be deduced from historical information. From the accounting system, the inflow of funds that the economy as a whole, a specific industry or a production technology generates over a period of time can be identified by adding up the inflow of funds from worker councils, manufactured capital and natural capital. This inflow can then be compared to total gross investments, or not yet depreciated capital assets, or total depreciations during the period, for the whole economy, the industry or the production technology in question and thus give an indication of the social return on investments (SROI).

Productive capital

Investments in manufactured capital can aim to replace depleted capital in an industry, i.e. replacement investments, or to increase the industry's productive capacity. When funds are used for investments, account *1.) Available* funds is credited. The relevant sub-account for industry in

INVESTMENT IN PRODUCTIVE CAPITAL	
Dr	Cr
4.a) Investment - productive capital	1.) Available funds

account category *4.a) Investment in productive capital* is charged.

An investment will also generate an entry in the accounting entity *Industry Federations' stocks of produced productive capital* as described earlier in this chapter.

Shared support resources, R&D and labour

Some support functions that may be provided and financed collectively can be shared by the whole economy such as the tasks that the Iteration Facilitation Board perform, while others may be industry-specific, for example the creation and provision of economic statistics and other analyses that facilitate decision making, and the coordination, implementation and monitoring of decisions and activities. Shared support units that perform such tasks require resources mainly in the form of different categories of labour.

The transfer of funds from any of the investment fund's units – national, industry or regional - to a support unit generates a debit entry in the relevant sub- account in account category *4.b) Investments - support units*. Account *1.) Available funds* is credited.

FUNDING OF SUPPORT UNITS	
Dr	Cr
4.b) Investments – support units	1.) Available funds

One important investment category is the economy's investments in different research and development projects. One way to organise R&D is to establish separate worker councils for product development, development of production technology, exploration of different kinds of natural resources, etc. that are subordinate to and co-operate with the individual industry federations.

A transfer of funds from the investment fund to an R&D unit is recorded as a debit entry in the sub- account identifying industry federation in the account category *4c) Investment in research and development*. Account *1.) Available funds* is credited.

INVESTMENT IN R&D	
Dr	Cr
4.c) Investments - R&D	1.) Available funds

When changes in productive capacity (extensions as well as reductions) for different sectors of the economy are planned and implemented, this of course also affects the future demand for different categories of labour. Society's investments in training and education must therefore be planned simultaneously with other long-term planning. Basic education is presumably handled and decided in consumer federations while some types of vocational training falls naturally under the responsibility of worker councils and their federations. It is also reasonable to assume that society will establish units with the responsibility to facilitate retraining of workers and to help workers moving between workplaces or jobs etc.

This completes our summary description of the five main categories of accounting entities in a participatory economy. Two different types of entities remain to be explained. These entities are not accounting entities in the same meaning as above, but rather a type of *reconciliation entities* which facilitate the "conversion" of some of the costs that worker councils are charged into consumption points that consumers use for consumption.

CONSUMPTION RIGHTS IN A PARTICIPATORY ECONOMY

Compensation for socially valuable work

In a participatory economy the fees that worker councils are charged for user rights to different categories of labour are *not* the same as members' compensation for work. The user right fee is a reflection of the opportunity cost of the labour and is determined, among other things, by the availability of and the demand for a particular category of labour, and the marginal benefit it produces. In contrast, the consumption points that a member of a worker council is assigned as compensation for work is based on the member's effort or sacrifice. In other words, there is no *direct* connection between the fees for user rights that a worker council are charged and the compensation that the council's individual members receive.

However, there has to be an indirect connection between the *total* user right fees for labour (and fees for emissions of pollutants) that worker councils are charged, and the total consumption points available to consumers in the economy as a whole. If we want the general average price level in the economy to be fairly constant during the annual planning procedure and between years, which will facilitate planning, the total amount of available consumption points in the economy need to be matched by the total user right fees (and fees for emissions) that are charged to the worker councils. If the total number of available consumption points exceed the total fees that worker councils are charged there will be price inflation. If the total number of available consumption points fall short of the total fees charged to worker councils there will be price deflation.

How are consumption points for accounting purposes created in a participatory economy? One way to visualise this process is to identify a separate **reconciliation entity for work compensation**, where fees for user rights regarding labour from all worker councils are converted to consumption points after which they are "repaid" to the worker councils for internal distribution between their members.

COMPILATION OF CHARGED FEES FOR USER RIGHTS TO LABOUR IN THE ECONOMY:
+ User Right Fee per hour & Hours - Labour Category A
+ User Right Fee per hour & Hours - Labour Category B
+ User Right Fee per hour & Hours - Labour Category C
...
Total sum
COMPILATION OF DISTRIBUTED CONSUMPTION POINTS TO WORKER COUNCILS:
+ Worker council A
+ Worker council B
+ Worker council C
...
Total sum

Figure 3.6. Reconciliation entity - work compensation

The Iteration Facilitation Board estimates the total user right fees for labour in the whole economy for next year based on growth forecasts and on decisions in the long term planning regarding for example the production and productivity development, consumption, investments and the expected supply of labour. The total user right fees for labour should reasonably well match the total amount of consumption points that the workers as a collective can receive as compensation for work. In other words, the average compensation for a worked hour in the economy as a whole (**the basic income per worked hour**), should match the average fee for user rights for an hour of labour *regardless of labour category* in the economy as a whole.

Before the distribution of consumption points to individual worker councils, the basic income per worked hour may be adjusted for differences in effort and sacrifice *between* workplaces, and possibly also for differences in the desirability of different tasks, based on rules that will be described in *Chapter 5: Work and production*. However, these adjustments should not affect the average compensation per hour *for the whole economy*. The allocation of consumption points to individual workplaces can then be based on their total number of worked hours. The individual workplace distributes its total allotted amount of consumption points between its members based on estimates of effort and sacrifice at work, in whatever way that they consider to be most fair.

Compensation for damage caused by pollution

The second external source of consumption points for consumers in a participatory economy is the compensation that members of so-called **Communities of Affected Parties** (CAP) receive for damage caused by worker councils' emissions of pollutants. These CAPs can be thought of as reconciliation entities where worker councils' fees for emissions are recorded, converted into consumption points and distributed to individual members based on rules that the CAP decide (see figure 3.7).

The Iteration Facilitation Board (or some other support unit connected to CAP) compiles and summarises all fees that worker councils are charged for different categories of emissions within a CAP. The total sum of such charges that is credited a CAP should match the total sum of consumption points distributed to its members, possibly with deduction of administrative costs. These allocated consumption points are added to the consumption points that individual members earn in their workplaces.

A CAP will need help from support units and R&D units to handle administrative tasks, such as providing a basis for assessing applications for membership into a CAP, assessing what substances cause damage to members, what damage is caused at different quantities of emissions (although it is the members themselves who ultimately make the decisions and "value" their damage), and calculating and allocating consumption points to members if it is decided that the allocation should be based on differences in the damage that members suffer. The cost of such support units and R&D units could be collectively financed in accordance to decisions in the National Consumer Federation, or alternatively from the inflow of fees to the CAP from the workplaces, or through a combination of both.

COMPILATION OF CHARGED FEES FOR POLLUTION CREDITED TO A CAP
+ Fee per unit & Quantity - Pollutant A
+ Fee per unit & Quantity - Pollutant B
+ Fee per unit & Quantity - Pollutant C
...
- Administration
Total sum
COMPILATION DISTRIBUTED CONSUMPTION POINTS TO MEMBERS IN CAP
+ Member A
+ Member B
+ Member C
...
Total sum

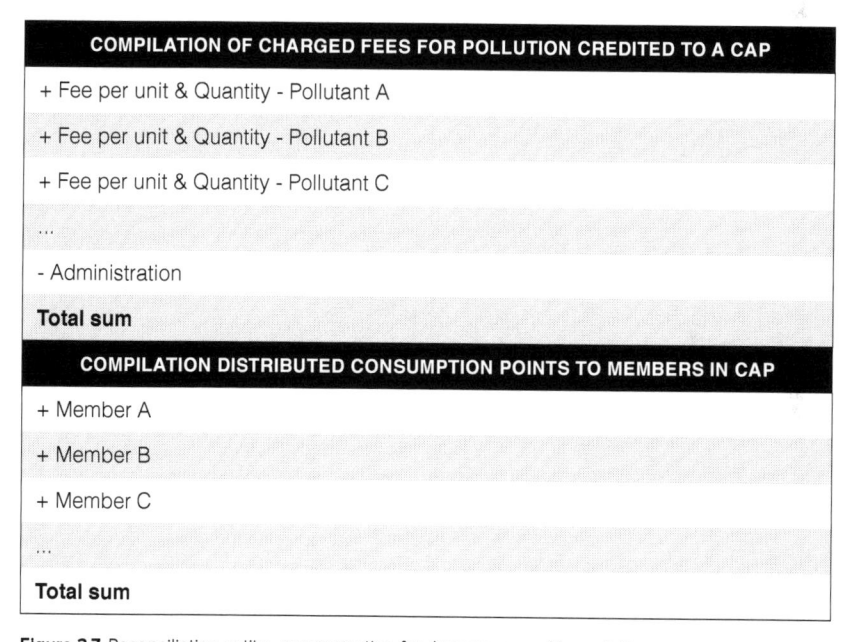

Figure 3.7. Reconciliation entity - compensation for damage caused by pollution

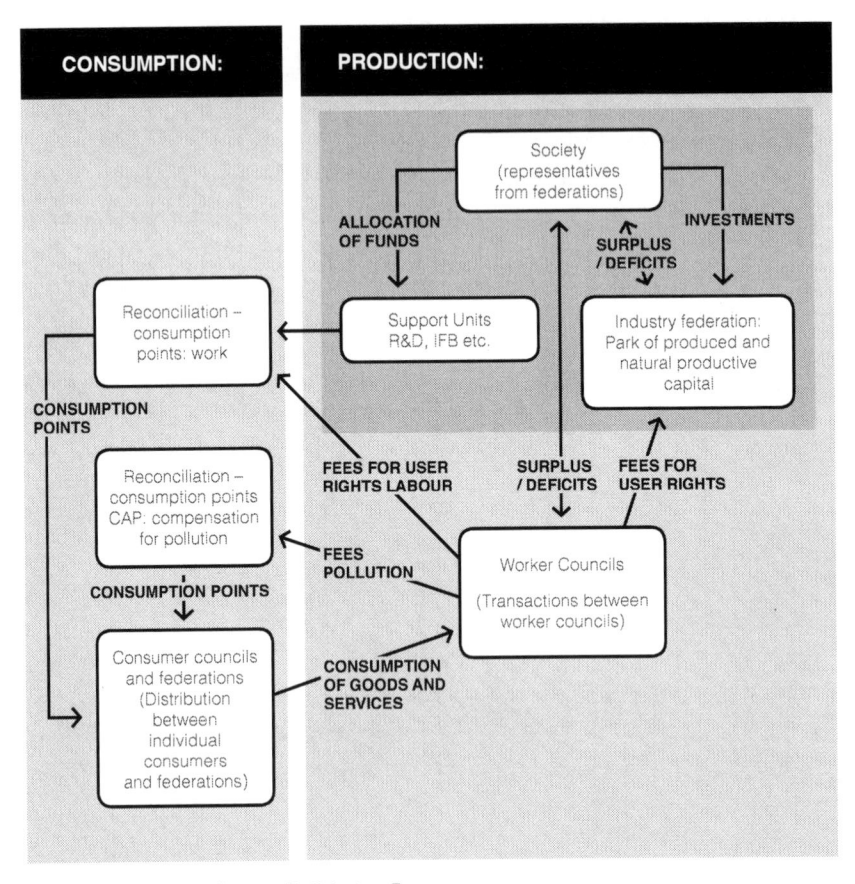

Figure 3.8. Transaction flow in a Participatory Economy

CHAPTER 4

CONSUMPTION

In a participatory economy, consumers have influence over the direction of production and its composition through the annual planning procedure, in which they announce their estimates of what they want to consume for the next year. The consumption proposals are revised by the consumers themselves during the annual planning in light of prices of goods and services, which are adjusted by the IFB before each new iteration based on excesses in supply and demand. It is important that the process of preparing and adjusting consumption proposals does not require too much time or is perceived as too cumbersome, and that approved proposals can be adjusted easily during the year if consumer preferences change.

In this chapter we discuss the planning, organisation and categorisation of consumption and how different consumption categories are recorded and monitored in our accounting system. Different aspects of the distribution of consumption points are discussed under the section on effort rating in *Chapter 5: Work and production* regarding compensation for work, and in *Chapter 7: The environment* regarding compensation for damage from pollution.

INDIVIDUAL CONSUMPTION AND THE CATEGORISATION OF GOODS AND SERVICES

Consumers' income and preferences change from year to year, and the main purpose of asking consumers to make proposals for what they expect to consume for the year ahead, during the annual planning procedure, is to make producers aware of these changes. The categorisation of goods and services in the proposals need not be particularly detailed for this purpose to be achieved. The proposals can be complemented with the necessary details based on consumer profiles and actual purchases as the year proceeds.

A consumer is expected to indicate her planned consumption for the upcoming year simply by entering her preferred quantity in front of a number of coarse categories of goods and services on a form. If she for whatever reason chooses not to do so, the Consumer Council, which she belongs to, can use her real consumption from the last completed year as her new consumption proposal for next year. If her planned allotment of consumption points for the upcoming year allows the previous year's level of consumption, the "proposal" can be approved and included in the Neighbourhood Council's overall proposal. If not, and if she continues to ignore requests for a new proposal, the Consumer Council can adjust the quantity for each category by the same percentage until the adjusted consumption proposal is covered by her available income. This way, the Consumer Council that is obliged to complete a consumption proposal for the entire neighbourhood, can fulfil its task even if some members do not submit individual consumption proposals. The councils may also adjust the total demand of individual goods in the annual planning procedure, based on their own calculations and forecasts, by proposing an increase or decrease in the distribution centres' inventories. Such adjustments in inventory for planning purposes may or may not be realised as the year progresses.

An individual consumption proposal is a consumer's best estimate of what she thinks she will consume in the upcoming year, based on a list of coarse categories of goods, for example, "shoes", "bicycles", "computers", etc. or even coarser categories. The task of categorising goods and services into coarse categories could be performed jointly by a categorisation committee made up of representatives from both consumer and worker federations; alternatively it could be decided to be a task solely for the National Consumer Federation.

In order to facilitate consumers' annual planning even further the consumer federation may in some cases and for some products create different "baskets" with sets of goods, the compositions of which are based on different consumer profiles and forecasts. In these cases, during the annual planning procedure the individual consumers will indicate which basket/consumer profile she prefers and in what quantity, instead of indicating her preference for each and every individual item. For instance, a vegetarian would indicate a basket of goods based on a vegetarian profile instead of specifying kilograms of carrots, bananas etc. Baskets may also be linked to the use of a specific good. For example, a holder of a certain type of car could be considered to automatically request a basket containing car accessories, spare parts, service etc. A basket of goods should reflect the expected average consumption pattern in the whole economy for a consumer profile. An individual consumer doesn't have to adjust her actual consumption to the composition of a basket but consume each constituent good individually during the year, since a basket's composition reflects the *average* in the whole economy. The consumer federation may adjust the baskets' compositions of goods during the annual planning procedure in light of changes in prices and other considerations.

The prices that the IFB announces in the planning procedure, and that consumers and worker councils base their proposals on, are *the average unit price* for a commodity in each coarse category. Each coarse category may contain a number of more or less detailed subcategories. Consumers will have access to information about the different variants of a product that exists and the characteristics that define each subcategory, in other words, the range of products that the producers are planning to offer. For instance, the coarse category "shoes" may contain sub-categories such as running shoes, casual shoes, smart shoes, sandals, etc. The creation of different sub-categories of goods in a coarse category is important for the producers when they plan their production and will be discussed in *chapter 5: Work and production*.

The price of different subcategories of a good in a coarse category can vary more or less sharply compared to the average price depending on differences in resource usage in the production, and a consumer must take this into account when she is planning her consumption for the year. When a consumer picks up an item from a distribution centre or uses a service, she is charged the *actual cost* (the price of the subcategory) of the product or service in question. A consumer who generally prefers more expensive varieties of goods and services will submit a consumption plan (based on average prices) for the coming year that underestimates the true total cost of her consumption. She will therefore tend to build up a debit balance - a debt - on her account as she consumes during the year. As long as this debt is kept on a reasonable level, there is no reason to believe that society will have any objections to this. A person who generally prefers cheaper varieties of goods and services will, on the other hand, tend to submit a consumption plan for the upcoming year which overestimates the cost of her total actual consumption, and she may therefore prepare and submit a *consumption proposal* which shows a debt that will never be realised in practice during the year.

Some consumers will be more accurate than others in preparing their consumption proposals, and other consumers will need to adjust their proposals during the year when their actual consumption deviates too much against the planned consumption. When a deviation exceeds a certain predetermined level, a consumer may be urged to update her consumption proposal. Adjustments of a plan during a year are recorded and followed by consumer and industry federations. Most adjustments will presumably cancel each other out at the total level in the consumer federations so that no, or only marginal, changes of production plans need to be made during a year. Small changes can be coordinated and handled through various IT tools that scan inventory balances. Major changes in consumption patterns during a year may require adjustments in existing production plans and prices, based on discussions and agreements between consumer and industry federations.

CONSUMER ACCOUNTS, COST CENTRES AND THEIR INTERNAL RELATIONS

Consumers' consumption plans and activities are recorded and followed in a structure of accounts that reflects the consumer councils' federation structure, which is built up from the bottom by separate accounts for each individual consumer or household. The diagram at the end of the chapter gives a schematic overview of the account structure and the internal relations between different accounts and cost centres in the consumer sector.

Individual accounts for consumers or households are organised in groups that are defined by the neighbourhood council to which the individuals belong. A neighbourhood council in turn has its own account for collective consumption, which is grouped together with accounts for other neighbourhood councils belonging to the same federation in the next level in the federation structure and so on all the way up to the national consumer federation.

Electronic cards, similar to today's credit or debit cards, may be linked to individual accounts in order to facilitate the registration of individual consumers' economic activities. If a consumer moves to a different neighbourhood consumer council, her account follows her.

The consumption points that an individual consumer receives as compensation for work in a worker council and for damage from emissions of pollutants, are credited to her individual account. Consumption points may then, after decisions in the neighbourhood council and/or the federations, be redistributed between different consumers' accounts, for example as transfers to those with special needs, and upward in the account structure to cover collective consumption at different levels of federations. Transfers of consumption points between consumers' accounts can be made on the basis of general national policy rules, such as a fixed amount to all who are older or younger than a certain age, or based on individual requests for additional allocations of consumption points for special needs. A transfer of consumption points upwards in the account structure for funding of collective consumption is done by charging an individual's account for her part of the collective consumption and simultaneously credit the receiving council's or federation's account with the same amount.

Allocation of costs to consumers

All costs for consumption of goods and services are distributed to accounts belonging to consumers, councils or federations via so called cost centres. Every cost centre belongs to a consumer council or federation. The cost centres serve as reconciliation objects for costs and constitute a "first stop" for all costs of goods, services, labour and resources that consumers consume, both individually and collectively. *All costs* that are charged to a cost centre are one way or another passed on to the different accounts of consumers, neighbourhood councils or federations, other cost centres or accounting entities.

COST CENTRE	
Dr	Cr
Social Costs:	**Distribution of costs:**
+ Goods/services	+ To individual consumers accounts
+ Emittance of pollutants	+ To accounts belonging to neighbourhood councils or federations
+ Use of labour	
+ Depreciation of capital assets	+ To other cost centres and accounting entities

Figure 4.1. A cost centre in the consumer sector

When it comes to consumption of individual goods it is the distribution centres or shops belonging to the neighbourhood councils that constitute cost centres. In the case of collective consumption it is the production units, i.e. the worker councils that produce and/or provide public goods such as education, health care, elderly care, etc. that, individually or in groups, constitute cost centres. As goods and resources are delivered and consumed, costs are passed on from cost centres to consumers' accounts in two principally different ways.

1. **Individual allocation:** Costs can be allocated from a cost centre to a consumer's account when an individual good or service is "picked up" or used, or via a calculated user fee associated with the use of a collective service or utility. The charge of a consumer's account reflects individual consumption, or individual utilisation of a collective service or utility. For example, when a consumer picks up groceries in a supermarket or buys a train ticket.

2. **Collective allocation:** Costs for an activity or service can be allocated from a cost centre to the account of a neighbourhood council or a federation. For example, when a neighbourhood installs swings and slides for a playground. In this case, the charge reflects the collective consumption of the council or federation, and individual members will be charged their portions of the cost by transfers of consumption points from their accounts to the council's or federation's account. The charges of individual members don't have to be the same for everybody but may instead aim to reflect differences in consumers' utilisation of a collective good. The councils and federations decide themselves how the allocation of costs for collective goods to their members will be done.

```
┌─────────────────┐              ┌─────────────────┐
│ Allocation at the│              │   Collective    │
│ time of delivery or│            │   allocation    │
│ usage (individual│              │  (collective    │
│  consumption)   │              │  consumption)   │
└─────────────────┘              └─────────────────┘
         ↓                                ↓
      ╱─────╲                         ╱─────╲
     │Individual│                    │Consumer council│
     │consumer │                     │ or federation │
      ╲─────╱                         ╲─────╱
```

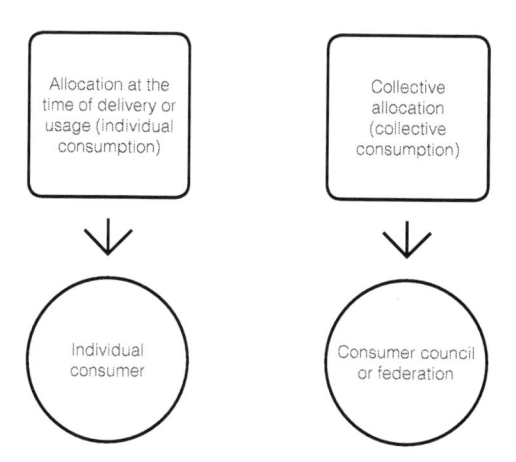

Figure 4.2. Allocation Principles: Consumption costs

A collectively provided service or a utility may thus be financed either through a calculated user fee at the time of individual usage, or via collective allocation where costs in the end are distributed to all members, or through a combination of the two.

A cost centre may simultaneously have costs that are distributed to consumers individually at the time of delivery or usage, and other costs that are allocated collectively to the councils/federations. Costs within a cost centre that are to be allocated with the same allocation principle are gathered in separate cost pools from which they are allocated to individual consumers, councils and/or federations.

If costs for the provision of a collective service or good are distributed to consumers via a user fee, the size of the fee needs to be calculated based on an estimated utilisation rate. The more expected users, the lower the fee since the costs can be distributed to a larger number of consumers. However, a council or federation can always subsidise a user fee by a collective cost allocation of a part of the costs. At year end, any difference between a cost centre's charged and allocated costs will be cleared against the consumer council or federation to which the cost centre belongs.

Furthermore, a collective service or good may be provided by several workplaces jointly, which needs to be considered when calculating the fee so that all relevant costs are included in the calculation. It is the members of the council (or federation) that ultimately are responsible for the calculation of user fees.

Finally, costs for collective goods and services that are allocated through user fees, for example certain infrastructure, may in some cases be allocated not only to consumers' accounts but also to the accounts of other accounting entities and cost centres, which use the utilities.

Liabilities and Savings

The consumption of individuals, consumer councils and federations is recorded in the relevant accounts in the account structure. During the annual planning the proposed quantities and costs of consumption of different categories of goods, services and resources may change from iteration to iteration. Once an annual plan has been accepted, planned consumption - quantity and cost - of every coarse category of good and service is registered in each individual's, consumer council's and federation's account, as well as their expected income.

As the year progresses, actual consumption - quantity and cost (now based on the more detailed subcategories of goods and services) - as well as actual income is recorded for each account, and compared with the plan. Any decided adjustments to the current plan are recorded.

When the year is over and all transactions have been recorded, some consumers, neighbourhood councils and federations will have a debit balance in their accounts since their charges for consumption will exceed their consumption points. Such a balance is a liability, a loan to be repaid through lower consumption in coming years. A debit balance is carried forward to the next year and thus reduces the room for consumption that year, and so on until there is no debt and no debit balance. A liability may be a planned loan that is formally approved by the neighbourhood council during the planning procedure, or it may be unplanned, for example due to consumption of more goods than planned, or goods whose costs exceed the average for the coarse category. Whatever the case, the result is that the consumer/household (or council or federation) will have to limit future consumption in order for future consumption proposals to be approved. The detailed rules for approvals and settlements of loans are decided by the neighbourhood council in question and is influenced by assessments of consumers' credibility.[24]

Some consumers, councils and federations, on the other hand, will show a credit balance since they did not use up all their available consumption points. Such credit balances can be interpreted as savings of income for future consumption. A credit balance is carried forward to the next year and thus increases the room for consumption that year.

NEIGHBOURHOOD COUNCIL/FEDERATION	
Dr	Cr
Consumption and transfers: + Transfers of consumption points to higher and lower federation levels and households + Costs for collective consumption: From cost centres + Debt from previous years	*Consumption points* + Transfers of consumption points from individual consumers and other councils + Savings from previous years

Figure 4.3. Account: Neighbourhood council or consumer federation

---

24 The equivalent of credit assessments of borrowers that banks and other private creditors make today when preparing loans.

INDIVIDUAL CONSUMER	
Dr	Cr
Consumption and transfers: + Transfers to neighbourhood councils and federations for redistribution of consumption points + Transfers to neighbourhood councils and federations for collective consumption + Costs for individual consumption and collective consumption financed by user fees: From cost centres + Debt from previous years	*Consumption points* + From work + From CAP + Transfers and reallocations + Savings from previous years

Figure 4.4. Account: Individual Consumer/household

THE PHYSICAL DISTRIBUTION OF GOODS

Distribution of goods and services in a participatory economy can of course be organised in many different ways with different types of distribution centres and stores. The neighbourhood councils make their own decisions about this, and about how costs for the distribution of goods should be financed. The costs associated with distribution of goods can be categorised as (a) operating or handling costs, for example labour costs for warehouse workers and store personnel, and "marketing"[25], and (b) capacity costs for fixed assets in the form of various categories of capital such as buildings and machines.

Costs for capital assets could be considered part of a cost pool to be financed collectively by all members in the consumer council irrespectively of the extent to which the distribution centre or store is utilised by various members, since these assets can be considered to belong to the neighbourhood's "infrastructure" (see later in this chapter for further discussion of infrastructure). Operating costs on the other hand perhaps should be financed by a fee charged to the consumers as a mark-up on

---

25 Note that it is the consumers in their distribution centres, councils and federations that are responsible for marketing and the information about available goods and services, and not the producers, which presumably leads to dramatically more objective and efficient product information.

the goods they pick up. In this way, the operating costs will be borne by the individual consumers based for example on the value of the goods they consume.

When a consumer picks up a good at the distribution centre her account is charged with the cost of the good, and with a mark-up to cover the operating costs of the distribution centre, calculated as a percentage of the cost of the good and/or based on weight or volume. The size of the mark-up could be calculated by the consumer council (or possibly the distribution centre) and may be modified during the annual planning procedure based on changes in volumes, but would be guaranteed by the consumer council during the year. The same amount that is charged to the individual consumer's account - the cost of the good plus a mark-up - is credited to the distribution centre's account.

A distribution centre doesn't need to pass on all costs for acquired goods to end consumers in the same period. Keeping stock means that some goods can be acquired in one period and distributed to consumers in a different future period. This in turn simply means that the distribution centre will show a debit balance corresponding to the value of the inventory at year end which will be carried forward to the next period.[26]

Consumer federations may, in solidarity or for other reasons, decide to equalise freight costs between different geographical areas within a region – between remote and hard to reach communities with higher actual freight costs and more centrally located and easily accessible communities with less shipping costs. Total shipping costs would then be allocated to delivered goods based on their weight or volume regardless of how far they have been transported. A freight centre can be charged all actual shipping costs within a region, and allocate these costs to receiving distribution centres via fees or a general mark-up percentage on the delivered goods. This way a good with the same weight or volume would bear the same freight costs regardless of where within the region it is consumed.

An important task for the consumer federations and the workers at distribution centres will be to function as "purchase departments" which

---

26 However, changes in an inventory balance need to be settled against the neighbourhood council account. An increase in an inventory balance is charged, and a decrease in an inventory balance is credited to the neighbourhood council account.

order, assess and approve deliveries of goods from worker councils, and manage what we today call 'warranty claims' for products that do not measure up. Categories of goods are classified in terms of different characteristics, materials and quality. In some cases it will presumably be relatively easy to determine if a product meets the established criteria, while in other cases it may be more difficult. Goods that are not accepted will be returned to the worker council. Consumer councils will probably also set up and offer different "insurance solutions" in order to deal with repairs of certain types of durable and expensive goods. Assessments of *services* with regard to the execution and time spent may prove more difficult. An important role for the consumer federations will therefore be to establish and fund routines and structures that will help individual consumers to judge and question the services rendered by worker councils.

TRADE WITH SECOND-HAND GOODS

A participatory economy needs, not least with regards to reducing our impact on the environment, to facilitate a smooth trade in used goods or second-hand goods, i.e. previously manufactured consumer goods that can still be used, and to do so in a manner that is consistent with the model's values. It is worth noting the risk of markets and/or competing currencies arising in connection with trade in used goods, which at least theoretically could lead to major negative consequences for income distribution, which in turn could potentially threaten the stability of a participatory economy. It is therefore important that this risk is considered and managed when trade in second hand goods is organised.

Second hand goods can in this context be defined as goods that have already been requested, produced and delivered in accordance with previous years' plans, and whose value exceeds a certain amount, and have a remaining economic life span exceeding a certain number of years. Examples of such products are cars, motorcycles, bicycles, certain types of furniture and television sets. Because second-hand goods are goods which have already been produced and delivered to a consumer in accordance with a previous year's plan, the organising of trade in such goods will primarily be an internal matter for the National Consumer Federation (NCF) and can be handled more or less separately, outside of the annual planning procedure. The worker councils will of course be affected by a well-functioning trade in second hand goods as demand for new varieties of the goods are affected - but this is only an indirect effect.

The accounting of trade with second-hand goods

There are several ways in which a trade of second-hand goods can be organised within the framework of the values of a participatory economy and the following is just one possibility.

Trade in second hand goods essentially means two things: firstly, a good is transferred between two consumers, and, secondly, consumption points are transferred between different consumer accounts. A consumer who sells a previously purchased good to the neighbourhood centre for second-hand goods is credited its value as compensation.

INDIVIDUAL CONSUMER - SALE OF USED GOODS	
Dr	Cr
	A. Credit entry for a used good sold by a consumer

The neighbourhood centre for second-hand goods (a cost centre) is charged the value of the good.

COST CENTRE: DISTRIBUTION CENTRE FOR SECOND-HAND GOODS - RECEIPT OF USED GOODS	
Dr	Cr
A. Charge for received second-hand good	

Consumers who collect, or purchase, a second-hand good from the neighbourhood's distribution centre for used goods pay with consumption points charged to their accounts, (B),

INDIVIDUAL CONSUMER - PURCHASE OF USED GOODS	
Dr	Cr
B. Charge for a second-hand good purchased by a consumer	

The centre for second-hand goods is credited with the same amount.

COST CENTRE: DISTRIBUTION CENTRE FOR SECOND-HAND GOODS - DELIVERY OF USED GOODS	
Dr	Cr
	B. Credit entry for a second-hand good purchased by a consumer

The re-allocation of second-hand goods between buyers and sellers who live in different geographical areas can be organised through the geographically increasingly larger consumer federations. The distribution centres that receive second-hand goods are responsible for making sure that the goods received are functional and meet a certain standard.[27] Only approved items qualify the seller for reimbursement.

Ultimately, the National Consumer Federation (NCF) acts both as a requesting party and as a supplier of second-hand goods. In order to make it easy for people to be able to decide if they want to purchase or submit a used item, the NCF may announce preliminary depreciation schedules for the available categories of second hand goods, which give people an idea of the amount they can expect to be reimbursed when submitting different second-hand goods in the upcoming year, and the amount that they can expect to be charged if purchasing a second hand good. The provisional depreciation plan could be updated before the start of every year based on assessments of excess supply and demand, but during the year the NCF would in this case guarantee the provisional prices for both buyers and sellers until the next update. This could result in a surplus or deficit from the trade in second hand goods for the NCF as a whole, which would accrue to all consumers in the economy. Alternatively, the NCF may adjust prices throughout the year so that supply meets demand for each category of second-hand good. This could eliminate surpluses and deficits in the NCF but would instead require adjustments in arrears of debit and credit entries in the individual buyers and sellers accounts.

Consumers are free to create alternative trade mechanisms for used goods outside the formal trade practices, but such alternative trade

---

27 Distribution centres for second hand goods will of course also have handling costs and may have to add a mark-up to price of a second hand good in order to cover administration and operating costs in the same manner as ordinary distribution centres.

mechanisms would of necessity be pure barter or have to be based on a new, rival currency that would not be viable for newly produced goods or services. Flea markets where goods with only a marginal value change hands could be an example of such trading. The risk of such private exchange system growing large should be small as long as the NCF's official system works well.

Collectibles

One category of second-hand goods that differs from other durable goods are collectibles, goods that mainly have a value to collectors and in our current economy often increase in value over time. It can be many different items, such as stamps, art objects, furniture, various antiques etc. In a participatory economy, people will not be able, or need to, "invest" in collectibles for return on capital, and because the income distribution will be considerably more equal, prices for collectibles will likely be far lower than today. But it is reasonable to assume that some people, even in a participatory economy, will want to collect various items. Collectibles could be classified based on the extent to which they are considered to have a public value for the whole society. Some items may have only a limited public value to society but a great value for a group of collectors, while other items may have a great value for both individual collectors and for society and therefore perhaps belong in a museum where everybody has access to them. If society wants to allow some limited type of "trade" with collectibles, the NCF will have to take an active role. It needs to decide which items belong in a museum as a result of large collective value, and therefore should be excluded from trade. Furthermore, the NCF must take the responsibility for setting repurchase prices in a way that prevents individuals from gaining unjust economic benefits. If this trade with collectibles generates a surplus it accrues to the NCF and thus to all consumers.

Finally, since inheritance is not consistent with economic justice, and therefore unlikely to be part of a participatory economy, a collector's item with a substantial value and not merely personal value, will return to society at the time of a collector's death. However, at the time of a person's death relatives could be offered first option to take over the possession of collectible item by paying the same amount to the NCF as any other party.

COLLECTIVE CONSUMPTION

Public goods are by definition available to all members on equal terms. *Collective consumption*, as we use the concept here, may also include services that are provided collectively by the neighbourhood council or federations, but whose operating costs are to be allocated to consumers, totally or in part, through individual user fees at the time of the utilisation of the service. Collective services may include services and utilities that society, a council or a federation want to make sure are available for all their members, including in regions or areas with a small consumer base, or services considered to be so important to the community or region that individual consumers should not be tempted to renounce them in favour of other consumption.

The members in every consumer council and federation need to think about which goods and services they want their councils and federations to provide collectively and how they should be funded - collectively or via user fees. Collectively funded consumption means less room for individual consumption and vice versa. The next step could be to discuss and decide the distribution of available resources among different public services and utilities. It is the task of the members in the councils and federations to decide what goods and services that should be collective, their internal prioritisation and their funding.

An efficient planning and management of collective consumption will presumably require that members in consumer councils and federations have access to an administrative organisation, subordinate to the councils and federations, which will prepare and facilitate decisions, implementation and monitoring of collective consumption. It could consist of separate entities with different responsibilities including healthcare, education, park management, power supply, etc. These administrative entities would themselves be worker councils whose resource assignment ultimately would be decided by the councils and federations.

Of course, it is the consumers themselves in their consumer councils that determine how the decision making procedures regarding collective consumption will look like. Different councils may have different requirements for data collection, preparatory meetings, public debates, etc., all of which would be organised throughout the year. But it is only in the annual planning procedure that resources are requested and allocated to different types of consumption, both individual and collective, and the consumption is approved by other councils. Consumer councils and federations may, just as individual consumers, change their collective consumption proposals between iterations in the annual planning procedure based on changes in prices on different resources.

The goods and services that consumers in their councils and federations decide should be collective (e.g., health care, elderly care, education, different categories of culture, public transportation, firefighting, postal services, park administration, etc.) are produced and provided by self-managed worker councils, which may organise themselves into federations to coordinate and manage their internal production issues, such as the planning and distribution of work assignments. Issues related to start-ups and closures of worker councils that produce collective services, however, should presumably be handled by the consumer councils. The reason for this division of responsibility is that the production of public services is often directly and intimately connected to the receiver or user of the service in a fundamentally different way, as compared to the production of goods. Long term relations and trust between the provider and receiver of the service are often of fundamental importance. It may sometimes even be hard to separate the production of a service from the consumption. It can therefore be argued, as we do, that it should be the consumers, possibly through their administrative entities, that ultimately control the start-ups and closures of worker councils that produce and provide collective services.

Worker councils that produce for collective consumption prepare and submit production proposals during the annual planning procedure, just like any other worker council, based on guidelines from the administrative entities belonging to the consumer councils, but presumably without separately quantifying the value of the social benefit of their production. It's the total *production cost* for collective consumption that in one way or another is distributed to consumers. Or in other words, once a consumer council or federation decides on the production of a collective good, the social benefit will per definition be equal to the production cost for the provision of the good. The production proposals during the annual planning, or rather the cost estimates in these cases, will instead make up the basis for decisions in the consumer councils and consumer federations regarding the allocation and funding of different types of collective consumption. The process is somewhat similar to an open tender situation today but note that from the perspective of the members in a self-managed worker council it is not about maximising profit, for example by minimising costs as today, but to seek a level of effort in relation to compensation that is perceived to be on par with or better than alternative job opportunities.

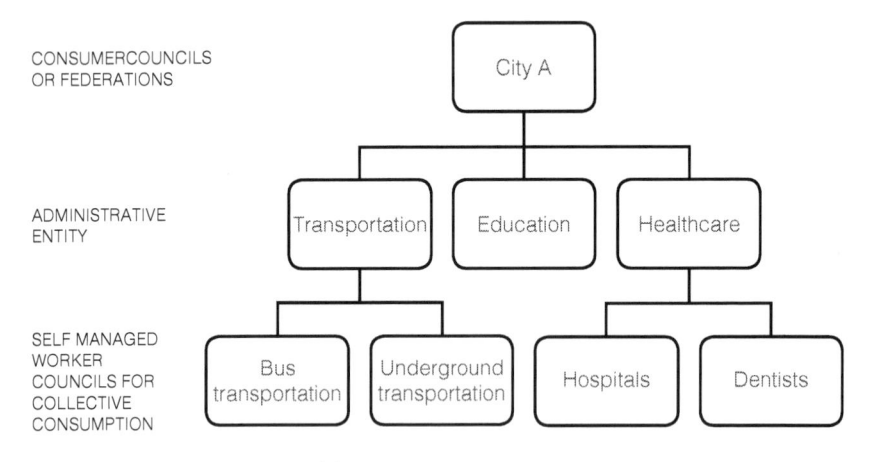

Figure 4.5. Collective consumption: Administrative organisation

COLLECTIVE CONSUMER INVESTMENTS

Costs for the production of collective goods and services can be divided into (a) running operating costs and (b) investments in productive capital assets. An investment in a capital asset with a long economic life span entails an expenditure at the time of acquisition after which no other disbursements are made during the asset's economic life. Costs for collective consumer investments will presumably, in principle, always be distributed collectively to the consumer council or federation, while the running operating costs for the provision of the service *may* be distributed to individual consumers through user fees.[28]

---

28   Another possible alternative could be to assign the running production of a collective good to worker councils on the producer side even though the investments are controlled and funded collectively by the consumer federations. The services would then by priced in the annual planning iterations.

In order to create good conditions for planning and decision making regarding collective consumption and consumer investments in the federations; (i) the worker councils who produce collective goods and services, and/or the relevant administrative entity, need to create a plan for required investments for the following years based on the desired production levels, and (ii) the acquisition costs for investments need to be distributed over the asset's economic life through depreciations, which will give an idea of how quickly the assets are consumed and how fast they will need to be replaced.

Acquisition costs of productive capital assets - buildings, machinery etc. - could be recorded in separate cost centres, where the rest value after deduction of accumulated depreciations is carried forward to future years until the rest value is zero.

COST CENTRE	
Dr	Cr
Investments: + Capital Investment A, B, C − Accumulated depreciation A, B, C (Cr)	**Allocation of expenses:** +/− Allocation of costs to Consumer Council or Federation

Figure 4.6. Cost Centre for capacity costs in an administrative entity

The annual depreciations will decrease the rest value of the assets, and will be charged to the cost centres for running operating costs, and will thereby be included in the costs that are allocated to consumers either by user fees or by collective allocation. With a *collective cost distribution*, the depreciations will increase the amount that is charged to the consumer council/federation which made the investment. With a cost distribution via user fees, it is the individual consumers in the council/federation that will be charged directly with the amount of depreciation through higher user fees.

The consumer collective as a whole should obviously not be charged both with the annual depreciation costs and the acquisition cost but only with latter, which means that the depreciations that are charged to the cost centres for running operation costs need to be "repaid" to the consumer federation. From the perspective of the consumer collective, the depreciation is only an allocation of the investment cost *between* consumers.[29] In appendix 3 we describe the accounting entries that are associated with collective consumer investments.

Consumer councils' and federations' available capital resources may of course be recorded and monitored in separate even more detailed asset registers, which identify each individual capital asset, its acquisition date, acquisition cost, economic life span, depreciation principles, accumulated depreciation and remaining undepreciated amount, and cost centre to which they belong.

EXAMPLES OF COLLECTIVE CONSUMPTION

Below we give a few examples of how collective activities could be organised and financed. It is worth to underline once again that it is the councils and federations that decide the features, scope and funding of the collective consumption, and the following should be viewed only as a discussion with a purpose to exemplify possible options to manage and fund various forms of collective consumption.

Research and Development

If consumers in a participatory economy want to gain influence over product development, they could, through their councils or federations, establish and collectively fund research and development units with the task of developing proposals for product specifications which could be discussed with the worker councils' industry organisations in preparation of their product planning. A special variant of such R&D units are units connected to groups of people who are affected by pollution, called Community of Affected Parties (CAPs) that are doing research on the effects of environmentally harmful emissions of pollutants. We will return to these CAP units in chapter 7: The Environment. R&D units are self-managed worker councils with limited or no decision making power over the decisions that their sponsoring consumer councils make, but who themselves decide on how to organise and run their own activities

---

29 Note the difference between "consumer investments" and "production investments". In the case of consumer investments it is about distributing the acquisition cost to consumers in a way, which they themselves decide. On the other hand, when worker councils use productive capital they are charged a fee for user rights which is decided by supply and demand during the annual planning procedure, and which reflects the opportunity cost for the usage of the capital asset.

using the resources and mandate assigned to them based on their production proposal.

Infrastructure

An important long-term issue for a society and its citizens, both in their capacity as workers and consumers, involves the shaping of society's infrastructure for communication and transportation. A well-developed infrastructure has a major impact on society's potential for efficient production and consumption. It is about the planning and development of road networks, railway lines, ports, airports and much more, and it involves major investments, the planning of which belong in the long-term development planning and investment planning where both workers and consumers participate.

The large group of investments and activities that together make up the infrastructure in the broadest sense includes many different categories of investments, some that will be classified as public necessities and funded collectively, and some that more directly will be considered part of the industry federations' capital investments and funded through the procedures relating to such investments. To illustrate the problem, we briefly discuss below some different approaches.

Costs for providing and maintaining society's road network could be considered part of a cost pool to be funded collectively by the members of society regardless of the degree of utilisation, alternatively with partial funding from industry federations through an annual fee on a collective level or the equivalent, following negotiations and decisions during the investment planning.

Maintenance of railroad networks, ports and airports *could* be part of a collective cost pool financed, wholly or partly, by user fees, while the initial investments i.e. capacity costs, might be financed collectively by the consumer and possibly also industry federations. The user fees for funding maintenance costs could be based on the number of transported kilometres (the railroad network), weight or volume units (ports) or departures (airports), and they would be charged to all worker councils that utilise the resources regardless of whether they provide services for collective or individual consumption, and regardless of whether they belong to a consumer federation or to an industry federation of producers. The user fees, or the rules for calculating them, could be decided collectively by the federations before each annual planning or by the IFB based on directives from the federations with the aim to cover all or part of the total estimated costs based on estimated capacity utilisation.

HOUSING AND COMMUNITY FACILITIES

One important and prominent task for the neighbourhood councils and federations is to plan, build, maintain and fund housing with associated community facilities such as garbage collection, water and sewer, playgrounds, parks, sports facilities, swimming pools, cinemas, cafés, restaurants and so on.

Housing

The planning of the construction of residential buildings as well as much of the community facilities need to be long-term and based on forecasts of changes in demographics and population. When a year starts the supply of housing is in principle fixed and a given. Housing is a collective consumption good that is planned and provided at the appropriate consumer federation level and the cost of construction and remodelling of housing would likely be considered collective investments and funded collectively.

Residents in a participatory economy would presumably not buy and privately own their housing in the same way as many do in today's society, but rather they will apply for the right to use a particular category of housing unit in a neighbourhood. Once they take residency of a housing unit they obtain the right to live there as long as they wish, assuming they fulfil their responsibilities, i.e. pay the established fee and act considerately towards their neighbours. It seems reasonable to assume that consumers in their consumer councils or federations will seek diversity in the supply of housing and residential areas. For example, people will want to be able to choose between different forms of housing, such as communal housing, apartments and free standing houses, depending on one's preferences and situation. Furthermore, it is inevitable that some homes will be more desirable based on location e.g. have better access to nice beaches, a coveted view and so on.

To allow for a fair allocation of housing the consumer council or its housing section/entity, first needs to classify the supply of housing in a number of separate categories defined by characteristics such as size, quality, access to the beach, view, and so on. The total operating costs of the worker councils responsible for managing the housing stocks, i.e. costs for management, maintenance and repair of the overall supply of housing within the federation, could be distributed to the residents via a housing fee per square meter living space. The fee may and will differ between housing categories but *the total aggregated housing fees should not generate any surplus*, only allocate the total costs to the residents.

The *base fee* for housing will thus be determined by the average cost per square meter for operating costs, management, maintenance and repairs for the total supply of housing in a region and will not change for any other reason than changed costs. The individual fee, on the other hand, can be adjusted in light of differences in demand for various housing categories. The consumer council could administer the allocation of housing via a housing agency subordinate to the Consumer Council's housing department, whose job it would be to help people find housing, and where people register their preferences for different housing categories. Based on the consumers' preferences, the individual fee can be adjusted by *the consumer council*, without affecting the average (base) fee, in order to change the demand so that the relationship between demand and supply for all housing categories will be similar. Differences between fees for different housing categories could help inform decisions regarding which housing categories to produce in the future.

From an accounting perspective, the housing fees would be handled in the same way as any other user fee, i.e. the consumer's account will be charged with the current fee for the category of living space that she has access to, and the same amount is credited the account of the housing managing worker council, which is responsible for operation, management, maintenance and repairs of the residential area in question.

Residents can without major difficulties be given influence over the development of their individual housing design, within the framework of general rules and definitions of different housing categories. Residents who want to be able to work on their houses or apartments, and thus to a larger extent design their homes can be given the opportunity to do so within the framework of the maintenance plans of the various housing categories. Maybe some housing categories should require a greater share of "own work" regarding maintenance and repairs, etc. which may be allowed to affect the calculation of the fee for the housing category. If the residents' own work replace maintenance and repairs *which normally is included* in the housing fees, the base fee before considering supply and demand could be adjusted proportionally.

Finally, it is reasonable that a resident will be guaranteed a fixed housing fee for a number of years before the next adjustment, and that family members of a resident who die are offered first option to take possession of the housing on payment of the current housing fee.

Community facilities

Community services or facilities, including services with a focus on leisure and entertainment, could be classified either as individually consumed services and priced through the annual planning procedure, or as collectively provided services that are funded collectively or through a calculated user fee.

A neighbourhood council or federation that wants to provide such services collectively may establish an entity in charge of the neighbourhood or municipality supply of restaurants, cinemas, theatres, etc. During the annual planning procedure, the council/federation could then calculate user fees that consumers are charged when they consume different categories of meals, visit the movies or the theatre, etc. that in the aggregate should cover all, or part of, society's total cost for providing the services. The fees for various activities could be updated by the consumer council during the planning procedure if prices for raw materials, forecast of capacity utilisation, etc. change.

Individual consumers would in any case specify in their consumption proposals how many visits to restaurants, the cinema, theatre, etc. they think they will make in the coming year. Individual consumers would be charged a fee every time they order a certain meal category at a restaurant, go to the cinema or theatre, etc. and the relevant worker council would be credited the same amount.

If a service is to be provided collectively, and primarily funded via a user fee, a portion of the fee *could be* subsidised by the council through collective funding if it is deemed desirable by the council's members e.g. if they want to favour a particular activity because it is considered to be positive for the neighbourhood. The neighbourhood council would also decide how detailed the categorisation of different activities should be. A more detailed categorisation creates opportunities to manage differences in demand due to qualitative differences between, say, seating in a sports stadium or at a theatre and so on, by differentiating the charges to reflect differences in quality.

CONSUMER FEDERATION	
DEBIT	CREDIT
Collective consumption, investments and transfers	Allocated consumption points

COST CENTRE: CAPACITY COSTS	
DEBIT	CREDIT
Social costs	Allocation of costs

↑ TRANSFER OF CONSUMPTION POINTS ↓

CONSUMER COUNCIL	
DEBIT	CREDIT
Collective consumption, investments and transfers	Allocated consumption points

COST CENTRE: CURRENT OPERATIONAL COSTS	
DEBIT	CREDIT
Social costs	Allocation of costs

↑ TRANSFER OF CONSUMPTION POINTS ↓

INDIVIDUAL CONSUMER	
DEBIT	CREDIT
Consumption and transfers	Consumption points

← CONSUMPTION POINTS FROM CAPS & WORK

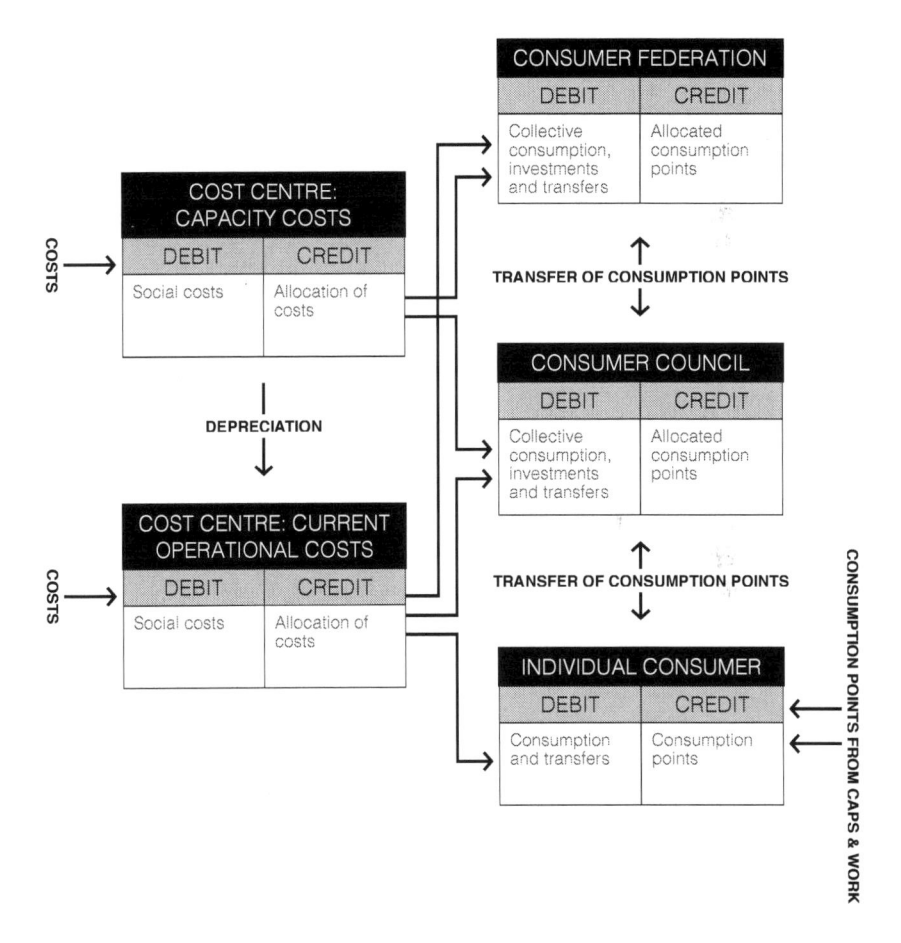

Figure 4.7. Consumer entities, cost centres, account structure and flows

CHAPTER 5

WORK AND PRODUCTION

Production in a participatory economy is carried out by self-managed worker councils who organise themselves into federations to manage decision-making affecting entire industries and to address long-term development and investment planning. During the annual planning procedure, the worker councils propose what inputs they need and the output they will produce, based on the prices that the IFB announces. The prices aim to establish a balance between supply and demand for all categories of capital, labour, intermediate and final products and services, and they therefore indicate opportunity costs for the use of capital assets and labour, and social costs for production of goods and services.

In this chapter, we discuss the categorisation of productive assets - manufactured and natural capital, and labour - with the aim to facilitate a correct valuation of the productive capacities of worker councils during the annual planning, i.e. a valuation that reflects opportunity costs. We then explain how the coarse categories of final products that are used in the annual planning can be broken down into more specific subcategories, so that producers can plan their production in an efficient and equitable manner, and what requirements this places on the accounting system.

But first of all we discuss different ways to cap the total income that a workplace will have access to for distribution to its members as compensation for work performed.

DISTRIBUTION OF CONSUMPTION POINTS

Every worker council in a participatory economy is expected to rate its members' efforts and sacrifices in the workplace using procedures, which itself designs and controls. The effort ratings then form the basis for the allocation of consumption points, as compensation for work performed, between members. The aim is that an average level of effort at work should result in an income that matches the average income in the economy. A greater effort should give a proportionally larger income, and less effort should result in a proportionally smaller compensation. Each individual worker council decides how detailed it wants to be when grading its members' efforts. Some worker councils may give all members the same effort rating for an hour worked, while other councils perhaps will establish committees that, guided by democratically decided procedures and rules, assess and evaluate their members' efforts to a high level of detail.

During the annual planning, consumers use estimates of their income to help plan their consumption for the year ahead. For obvious reasons, this figure is preliminary and, regarding income from work, largely based on members' intentions for the upcoming year with respect to their level of effort, which due to various reasons may change during the year. When an annual plan has been accepted, a member's expected earned consumption points based on the preliminary effort rating is recorded in the member's account. Throughout the year actual earned income is then recorded and compared to plan.

Capping of worker councils' access to consumption points

Although an individual workplace has complete freedom to design its own internal procedures for grading its members' efforts for the purpose of distributing income between its members, its access to *total* consumption points must somehow be related to other workplaces in the economy. The capping of a worker councils average effort rating, and therefore its members' compensation, relative to other worker councils in the economy can be done in two different ways, each with their own advantages and disadvantages.

Capping Rule 1: Based on SB/SC ratio

The first possibility is to cap a workplace average effort rating for a year based on how its ratio between credited social benefits and charged social costs (SB/SC) compares to other workplaces. For example, if a workplace's SB/SC ratio is 105% while the average for the industry (or for some other possible grouping of workplaces) is 100%, this means that the workplace average effort rating cap should be 105% (calculated as 105/100) of the industry average. This capping rule is based on the assumption that a higher SB/SC ratio actually indicates a larger effort by the worker council's members compared to the other workplaces, and that a better outcome cannot be attributed to other factors, such as more efficient machines. The annual planning procedure is designed to achieve this by pricing access to more efficient equipment and resources higher than access to less efficient equipment and resources. Thus, the denominator of the SB/SC ratio will be higher if more efficient resources are used leading to a lower SB/SC ratio at unchanged production quantity. If the annual planning procedure to a sufficient extent succeeds in this regard, the capping of the average effort rating based on worker councils SB/SC ratio will be fair.

In this context, the SB/SC ratios are *always* calculated based on actual outcome for the last completed year, and *not* on the preliminary proposals for the coming year prepared in the planning procedure. A relatively low SB/SC ratio for a worker council therefore means not only a lower average income for the members next year, but presumably also a problem with retaining and recruiting members because other worker councils with higher SB/SC ratios can offer a relatively higher average compensation for the next year. Worker councils therefore have an incentive to strive for a good outcome and not become complacent once their production proposal during the annual planning has been approved.

If there is a risk that the pricing of user right fees for capital, resources and labour in the participatory planning procedure not quickly or accurately enough reflect differences in efficiency and quality, it can be argued that capping of effort levels based on worker councils SB/SC ratios is unfair. Worker councils using relatively inefficient machines and resources would then be unfairly disadvantaged.

Capping Rule 2: An equal cap for all

The second rule for capping average effort ratings in workplaces means that all workplaces are considered to be equal in terms of average effort. No workplace can thus differ from any other regarding average effort grading. Using this alternative, one instead risks disadvantaging workplaces whose members are sincerely committed to more than average efforts. This rule may possibly be combined with a requirement for worker councils to demonstrate a certain minimum level of SB/SC ratio in order to be assigned the economy's average effort rating. If they fail to reach the required minimum SB/SC ratio, their average effort rating for the next year could be adjusted downwards by a certain percentage.

Choosing which capping rule to use

The choice and implementation of a capping rule does not necessarily need to be applied universally to all workplaces in the economy. For example, one industry could apply capping rule one, and another industry could apply capping rule two. Conditions may vary across industries in ways that hamper or impede the possibility for a fair comparison of SB/SC ratios between workplaces in different industries, even though comparisons between workplaces within the same industry are fair.

There may be other industry specific circumstances that make different industries more or less suited for using the capping rule based on the SB/SC ratios. For example, it is reasonable to assume that the *average effort* in worker councils belonging to industries with large production units are relatively equal since a large number of members equalises differences in average calculations. In such industries, it is perhaps justified that all councils are assigned the same maximum average level of effort rating. On the other hand, in industries where the production units are small, it may be more important to base the capping of effort rating on SB/SC ratios since it is likely that there are real differences in average effort between production units.

Furthermore, it is difficult to use SB/SC ratios as the capping rule for worker councils that produce for collective consumption or for shared support units where the social benefit of the production in principle is determined by the social cost. All this suggests that the capping rule preferably should be implemented by industry (or even by sectors of industry in some cases) and not for all workplaces generally in the economy.

Allocation of consumption points to workplaces

As described in chapter 3, a basic income per worked hour for the economy as a whole is calculated in preparation for the annual planning procedure. The basic income may need to be adjusted for different work tasks or different industries, to reflect that work tasks are more or less desirable or pleasant, and it may be impossible to sufficiently equalise these differences when jobs are balanced in the workplaces. If there are no such adjustments made, it may be difficult to find workers who want to perform certain undesirable tasks in the economy. However, the average income per worked hour in the economy as a whole should not be affected by these adjustments. Adjustments of the basic income per hour for relative desirability is about planning and "shaping" the supply of labour so that it has a chance to meet demand, which is a task for the long term planning. We will return to this task in the next chapter.

When the basic income per worked hour in the economy has been set, the IFB can allocate the consumption points to workplaces based on total number of worked hours, considering the chosen capping rule.

If applying capping rule 1, a workplace SB/SC ratio is compared to the corresponding ratio for the whole reference group and the number of received consumption points are adjusted accordingly. A reference group consists of all workplaces whose average incomes, according to the agreed capping rule, are to be decided based on their internal relative SB/SC ratios. A reference group could be made up of all the workplaces across several industries, in one industry, or in only one sector of an industry. It's the *workplace* actual SB/SC ratio for the previous year that is the basis for comparison, *but based on the current planning year's suggested number of worked hours.*[30]

Calculated basic income per worked hour × Worker council's worked hours × SB/SC of worker council divided by SB/SC of reference group (previous year) = Worker council's total income before adjustment for desirability

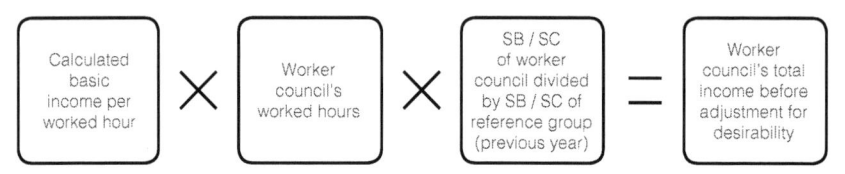

Figure 5.1. Capping rule 1: Allocation of consumption points to workplaces "Based on SB/SC ratio"

If applying capping rule 2, the estimated basic income per worked hour is simply multiplied by the proposed number of hours worked in the workplace.

Calculated basic income per worked hour × Worker council's worked hours = Worker council's total income before adjustment for desirability

Figure 5.2. Capping rule 2: Allocation of consumption points to workplaces according to "Equal caps for all"

WORKER COUNCILS' PRODUCTIVE CAPACITY

One important and crucial task for an accounting system in a participatory economy is to define and quantify the worker councils' unique productive capacities. A worker council's productive capacity is in simple terms defined by its members' training and skills, and the productive assets that

---

30 It is the workplace that is assigned the cap of average effort level, not the individual worker, which means that the reference group's average SB/SC ratio may (theoretically) change during the annual planning if the production proposals suggest that a large number of workers will move between workplaces with large relative differences in SB/SC ratios.

the council has access to, for example land, machinery and tools. Every worker council has access to a unique set of physical productive assets and a unique group of members, and hence has a unique productive capacity. Since the worker councils' production proposals are assessed and compared based on SB/SC ratios, the accounting system must identify and quantify differences in productive capacities for different worker councils in order for the comparisons to be fair. A higher productive capacity means higher requirements on delivered social benefit.

The prices for user rights for different categories of labour and capital that emerge in the participatory planning procedure play a crucial role when worker councils' productive capacities are estimated and compared. The goal is for the prices to reflect the opportunity cost of using different categories of labour and capital. To achieve this, and make the comparison of different production proposals fair, the categorisation of capital assets and labour must facilitate a pricing that reflects differences in capacity and productivity. A category of labour or capital with a higher productivity should be more expensive to use than one with a lower productivity.

Obviously, it is not possible to capture and quantify all factors affecting the productivity of resources. For instance, we cannot quantify and measure the effect of better or worse social relations in the workplace which may have a major impact on productivity. But with a well thought-out categorisation of capital assets and labour, the chances increase for a fair and efficient estimation of worker councils' production capacity.

MANUFACTURED CAPITAL

In the investment planning, which precedes the annual planning, representatives from industry federations (and consumer federations) make decisions about the economy's future productive capacity and thus also about what investments in productive capital (e.g. buildings, machines, equipment, etc.,) to make in the upcoming year. The productive capital available to industries in a year is, in other words, given and fixed when the annual planning procedure begins. The investment planning does *not*, however, determine how the user rights to existing productive capital will be allocated among individual worker councils. This is decided during the annual planning procedure.

Every worker council belongs to an industry federation based on what it produces. The grouping of worker councils into industry federations and sub-federations is described in the next chapter and may constitute a first basis for categorisation of productive manufactured capital - a first categorisation dimension. All capital assets that belong to a particular industry/production technology will then need to be categorised with respect to their function. Buildings, equipment and all other production equipment are classified according to their purpose and function, which is a second categorisation dimension. Finally, every category based on function needs to be classified in yet another level of sub categories based on capacity and productivity. Differences in capacity or productivity may be due to technological development between "generations" of machines or simply adaptations of machines and equipment due to special and differing needs.

All manufactured productive capital that exists in the economy, and their acquisition costs, are thus according to this model classified into categories based on a hierarchy of three different dimensions, (a) industry/technology (b) function and purpose, and (c) capacity and productivity. The point is that all assets in a category of capital should be as similar as possible in terms of functionality and capacity so that their user right fees as determined by supply and demand during the annual planning will reflect the opportunity cost as accurately as possible. It is the industry federations themselves that determine the boundaries and precise definitions of different categories of capital, perhaps as part of the investment planning. In other words, they decide how detailed the different capital categories should be, in order to promote as precisely as possible the estimates of the opportunity costs in the annual planning procedure, without creating too cumbersome an administration. A category of capital may consist of only one machine, factory building or plant e.g. a mining facility whose production capacity is unique and not comparable to other facilities in the industry, or it may consist of all available units of a capital asset with similar capacities in an industry e.g. all comparable fork lift trucks, lathes or assembly robots.

CATEGORISATION OF MANUFACTURED CAPITAL	
Dimension 1	Industry/Technology
Dimension 2	Function/Purpose
Dimension 3	Capacity/Productivity

The difference between investments and operating costs

In this context, there are two classification issues, which are important from a technical accounting perspective. During the investment planning procedure, the economy needs to define which expenses constitute investments and should be classified according to the schedule above, and which expenses that instead should be considered to be current operating costs.

A first classification problem is about the resources' economic life spans and acquisition costs. It is only meaningful to classify a productive resource as a capital asset in the way described above if it has a useful economic life span exceeding a certain number of years, and if its acquisition cost exceeds a certain amount. Expenses for productive resources with a short economic life span and/or with a low value should primarily be considered a current operating cost for worker councils. If this entails a risk of major incorrect accruals of costs between years, for example due to large purchase quantities of a low priced resource, the worker councils can accrue costs with the help of accrual accounts as described in appendix 2.

The second classification problem is about the distinction between investments and expenses for maintenance/repair of existing capital assets. Maintenance and repairs refer to activities that aim to prevent damage and to maintain existing assets' functionality and capacity, or to restore existing capital assets to their original standard in these respects. Maintenance are planned activities, and repairs refer to unforeseen measures. An investment, on the other hand, replaces worn-out assets, creates new productive capacity or improves production quality. Furthermore, a capital asset - a building, a machine, equipment, etc. - is in many cases made up of multiple sub-components that in themselves may have long economic life spans and be expensive to produce. Expenses for such components should not always be seen as investments when they need to be replaced but as a repair or maintenance cost for the industry federation or in some cases as a current operating cost for the worker councils. We return below to how such costs can be handled in a way that takes into account the various capital categories' different needs of maintenance and repairs.

Pricing of user rights

During the annual planning procedure, the rights to use productive capital is distributed to different worker councils. Every worker council identifies, as part of its production proposal, which parts of society's stock of capital, categorised as above, that it wishes to get access to. In their proposals the worker councils start with the capital assets that they already use - their initial set of capital - and then identify the capital assets they want to add, and the capital assets they no longer want or need. Note that different types of capital assets will be transferable to different degrees. Factory buildings and plants are examples of fixed or permanent assets that cannot be easily transferred between workplaces, and whose physical location, i.e. the workplaces to which they belong, presumably will be decided in the investment planning procedure, while machines and tools to different degrees can be transferred between workplaces. Changes in a worker council's set of capital assets may give rise to additional costs for the worker council in the form of set-up costs, training and restructuring of work routines etc. that the council needs to consider in its production proposal.[31] Other councils approve or reject a worker council's production proposal including its requests for access to capital assets, based on its SB/SC ratio as explained earlier. In each new iteration the worker councils can adjust their proposals regarding access to productive assets in light of changes in prices and other circumstances.

In the planning procedure the more productive capital assets will meet a higher demand and be assigned a higher user right fee per unit compared to the less productive assets. The result is that a worker council that intends to use relatively more productive assets will need to produce more social benefit than a worker council that plans to use relatively less productive assets, in order to get its production proposals accepted by the other worker councils. The pricing will thus reflect the opportunity cost of different productive assets in the economy.

The IFB's pricing of user rights for different categories of manufactured capital during the annual planning could computationally start with the depreciations of the assets' acquisition costs.[32] The acquisition

---

31 Reallocation of an economy's available capital resources among worker councils according to the accepted annual plan will furthermore take some time to execute, and a worker council will obviously not be charged any user right fees until an installation is complete. During the annual planning procedure the worker councils will need to know the expected installation dates for different capital assets in order to prepare production proposals. A capital asset's expected installation date should reflect the estimated *average* installation date in the economy for all installations of assets in the capital asset category.

32 The acquisition costs for productive capital assets are recorded in the accounting entities for the industries' stocks of productive capital.

costs (transportation and installation costs included) are depreciated at a rate that is determined by the industry federations in the investment planning and should reflect the assets expected economic lifespan. An asset's economic life span is in turn largely determined by (i) costs for repair and maintenance which increase with usage and age and eventually make newer versions economically preferable, and (ii) the rate of technology development for different capital categories. The faster the technology development rate for a category of capital, the shorter the economic life span and the faster the rate of depreciation as newer and better versions become available at a faster rate, making older versions obsolete. The average depreciation cost per unit for each category of capital in the economy may constitute a "base price" for the user right to one unit in each category which then can be adjusted during the annual planning procedure until demand meets supply for every capital category. The user right fees for fixed, non-transferable assets will presumably approximate the base price since these assets will not be "traded" to the same degree as more moveable assets.

| Average Depreciation Cost per unit in capital category X | × | Percentage adjustment to reach balance between supply and demand for capital category X | = | Price for user right to one unit of capital category X |

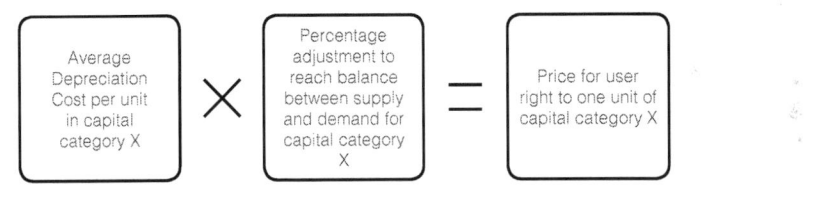

Figure 5.3. Pricing Model - user rights for a category of capital during the annual planning

The worker councils' need of repair and maintenance of capital assets is affected both by factors that largely can be predicted, for example, design, age and usage, and by factors that are difficult to predict, such as accidents or natural disasters. An industry may choose to collectively distribute certain unforeseeable expenses for repairs to all worker councils who use a certain category of capital assets through different "insurance solutions". The worker councils may then, by industry, be charged an "insurance premium" per unit of capital category they use, which in total will cover the industry's total estimated repair costs due to unforeseen events. The worker council's insurance fee would in this case entitle the council to repairs of damaged capital assets without any other charges. This way, the industry can reduce the impact of chance on the councils' costs and increase the degree of fairness.

Repair and maintenance costs that instead are caused mainly by outdated design or usage can be handled in, at least, two different ways.[33] An industry may choose to let its worker councils be charged the actual repair and maintenance costs. Worker councils will then have to consider these costs when they ask for access to different categories of capital during the annual planning procedure. This should work well enough if the expected repair and maintenance costs occur with short intervals and don't differ too much among different assets within the same capital category. If the capital categories manage to distinguish between capital with different repair and maintenance needs, it will presumably mean that capital categories with higher expected maintenance costs will get a relatively lower user right fee, and capital categories with less expected maintenance costs will get a relatively higher user right fee, everything else equal.

Alternatively, if costs for repair and maintenance are expected to occur irregularly and long between or if it is difficult to distinguish between assets with different needs for repair and maintenance when categorising capital, it may be more efficient and fair if these costs are covered (fully or partially) by the user right fees that worker councils are charged for access to different capital categories. For example, this may be relevant for certain long term fixed assets such as factory buildings and plants. The fee would then be calculated basically in the same way as described above, but the starting point for the calculation would now include both the average depreciation cost and the expected average maintenance and repair costs due to foreseeable factors, per capital unit for the capital category in the economy as a whole:

| Average Depreciation Cost + MAINTENANCE COST per unit in capital category X | × | Percentage adjustment to reach balance between supply and demand for capital category X | = | Price for user right one unit of capital category X |

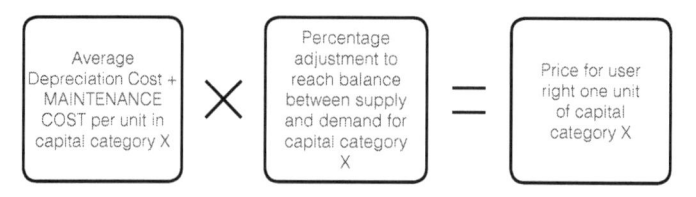

Figure 5.4. Pricing Model - user rights including (all or part of) maintenance costs for a category of capital during the annual planning

---

33   Increasing maintenance costs due to age and wear and tear is also considered when deciding the rate of depreciation of different capital categories, as noted above.

When a worker council initiates or performs maintenance work on capital assets during a year, for example by replacing worn components, the accounting entity for *the industry federation's stock of manufactured capital assets* would in this case be charged for the costs, not the worker council.

NATURAL CAPITAL

Resources that are provided by nature and neither can nor need to be manufactured are called natural resources. Some natural resources are easily accessible and basically inexhaustible, such as sunlight and wind, and are therefore not interesting from an accounting perspective. Other resources are productive, renewable and give recurrent return if they are cultivated sensibly, such as fertile agricultural land and forests. A third type of natural resources consists of non-renewable resources such as mineral, coal and oil deposits. In addition to not being renewable, the extraction of these resources often require large investments in costly fixed installations and manufactured productive assets, such as mining facilities and oil rigs or platforms, which means that it is difficult to separate such natural resources from the manufactured capital that is needed for the extraction. The installations, and fixed produced assets and the natural resource become one unit, the productivity of which is determined both by the design of the installations and the nature of the natural resource. Such installations for the extraction of natural resources may need to be classified as separate categories of capital in the annual planning if their productive capacity relative invested capital is unique.

We focus here on the second type of natural resources, which we call productive natural capital. Natural capital need to be categorised based on function and purpose in a similar way as for manufactured capital. During the investment planning the industries using natural capital, together with the other actors in the economy, will decide which natural assets that will be made available to industries in the coming years and what technologies that should be employed when cultivating them. In addition to industry and function, the industry federations need to classify natural capital assets with respect to fertility and return, through a categorisation schedule of their choice. In this case, as well, it is the industries themselves that decide the exact definitions of capital categories and their level of detail, presumably during the investment planning. The more accurate and detailed classification and categorisation of assets, the more exact will the pricing of user right fees reflect the opportunity costs. Since some of these assets' rate of return, or productivity, is affected by the level of utilisation, they may need to be reclassified with regard to fertility at regular intervals as they are used.

CATEGORISATION OF NATURAL CAPITAL	
Dimension 1	Industry/Technology
Dimension 2	Function/Purpose
Dimension 3	Soil Fertility/Return

The prices of user right fees for different categories of natural capital is determined in the annual planning procedure by the worker councils' demand for different categories and the existing supply. Categories of natural capital of high-quality and high-yield, the use of which require few and/or cheap resources will have a relatively high demand and thus be assigned a relatively high user right fee, whereas categories of natural capital of low quality that provide a low yield, and/or the use of which requires using a greater quantity or more expensive resources, will have little demand and be assigned a relatively low user right fee. The user right fees will therefore reflect the opportunity cost of using different categories of natural capital.

LABOUR

The supply of labour and the composition of different labour categories (e.g. plumbers, chefs, accountants, etc.) need to be adapted, as best as possible, to the long-term decisions about the development of the economy and its industries. In the next chapter we will look at what tools there are for the economy to shape the supply of labour. At this point we confine ourselves to noting that the labour supply and its composition of different labour categories in principle is given and fixed for the economy when the annual planning procedure begins.

As previously described, there is no direct link between the fees that worker councils are charged for access to different categories of labour and the compensation that members of worker councils receive for work. Since labour is a productive resource that together with the worker councils' access to manufactured and natural capital defines the productive capacity of the individual worker council, it is important that the user right fees for different categories of labour is priced in a way that as accurately as possible reflects labour opportunity costs. This means that labour, just like with any other type of productive capital, also needs to be categorised based on function and productivity.

The task of defining labour categories based on function will be affected by a participatory economy's ambitions to balance jobs with respect to empowerment and desirability, but also the economy's need for specialist and expert knowledge to promote efficiency. Furthermore, the categorisation of labour will have a major impact on the design of society's education system, both in schools and universities, as well as for vocational training. In other words, the task of defining labour categories is something that affects a large part of society and therefore presumably should be handled at a general level, for example during the long-term development planning and investment planning. To capture differences in productivity, each function category of labour may be divided into sub-categories based on labour experience and training so that labour with an experience/training that exceeds Y years form a separate sub-category of function category X, and labour with an experience that is less than Y years form another subcategory.

THE CATEGORISATION OF LABOUR	
Dimension 1	Function
Dimension 2	Experience/Training

In the annual planning procedure the worker councils ask for different categories of labour, and workers offer to provide labour in optional job categories. Note that a worker may qualify for more than one job category and that her choice of labour category may be influenced by compensation adjustments for less desirable job categories. The user right fees for labour categories that show excess demand are adjusted upward by the IFB, and the fees for user rights to labour categories that show excess supply is adjusted downward, until no excess demand or excess supply remain for any labour category. The user right fees will thus correspond to the opportunity costs of different labour categories.

The user right fees for different labour categories that the IFB announces and updates during the annual planning procedure are derived from the supply and demand in the economy as a whole, which means that there can be local and regional imbalances between supply and demand regarding different labour categories. Neither demand nor supply of various labour categories are evenly spread throughout an economy's geographical area. Some work tasks are for obvious reasons concentrated to specific areas, such as tasks within the mining industry or port operations, and other industries may for different reasons choose to allocate their production units to specific areas. Furthermore, the allocation of the supply of different labour categories to certain areas may depend on factors, such as the location of education facilities, or on historical or traditional reasons. In order to minimise local and regional imbalances between supply and demand of labour society may provide help and support to workers who want to change jobs or place of residence, or who want to retrain for a new job. This way workers freedom of choice can be maximised but also the supply of labour be made flexible and meet the demand. We will return to this issue in the next chapter which focuses on long term planning.

THE PRODUCTION OF GOODS AND SERVICES

Above we have focused on the categorisation and pricing of user rights to society's productive resources. We will now proceed to discuss the categorisation and pricing of the goods and services that are produced using these productive resources.

Categorisation of products

The production of productive capital resources (to be distinguished from the use of them) is a special case and is discussed in the next chapter. Other goods can be divided into final products, which are intended to be consumed by end users, and intermediate goods that in one way or another are part of the production of final products. Our focus in this section is mainly on final products but what is said below is in principle applicable to all types of products and services.

We have already noted that the needs and demands regarding the categorisation of goods and services produced for end consumption differ depending on whether one is a producer or a consumer. As we described in chapter 4, we want consumers to be able to influence what is produced in the economy by indicating preferences in consumption proposals during the annual planning. But we want them to be able to do this as smoothly and easily as possible without having to spend an excessive amount of time, which among other things means that the categories of goods and services used in consumption planning should be few and based on function in a broad sense. The categories of goods should in other words be "coarse" with as few details as possible. The producers, on the other hand, when preparing their production proposals need a more detailed categorisation of goods and services indicating differences in potential resource usage in the production of different varieties of products.

This difference in producer and consumer demands on the categorisation of goods can be managed by working with *both* a relatively small number of *coarse main categories*, which are the categories that consumers base their consumption plans on and worker councils relate to when assessing demand trends, AND at the same time a number of *more detailed subcategories* of products, every one of which belongs to a main category and is defined based on differences in potential resource usage in production. The more detailed subcategories will help worker councils to plan their need for various resources and inputs in their production. This double categorisation means that every product will belong to both a main category *and* a subcategory.

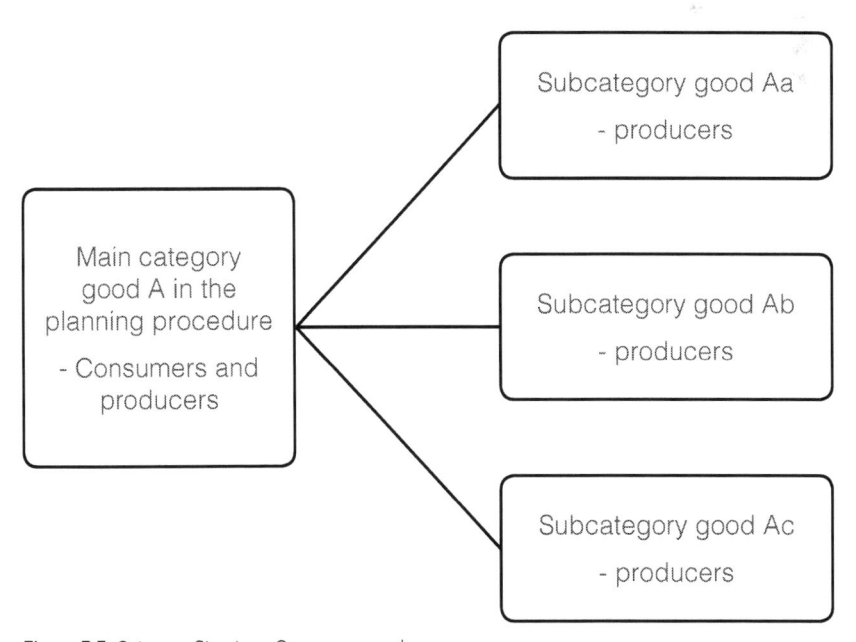

Figure 5.5. Category Structure: Consumer goods

It is the coarse categories of goods that are priced by the IFB in the annual planning procedure based on supply and demand. The more detailed subcategories may be created and defined by the worker councils themselves in their industry federations, possibly with the consideration of information and requests from consumer federations. The subcategories may be more or less detailed. The more detailed they are, the better conditions for producers to plan their production in an efficient manner, which also leads to a more accurate pricing of the main categories.[34] At the same time, administrative costs risk becoming large with an overly detailed categorisation of products, for instance due to increased costs for making sure that goods fulfil the defining criteria of subcategories.

The set of subcategories can be thought of as the range of products in a main category that will be available to consumers to choose from. We can, for example, imagine that the main category "Shoes" - the category for which consumers indicate their planned consumption during the annual planning - is divided into a number of subcategories such as men's and women's shoes of course, but also dress shoes, casual shoes, trainers, boots, etc. where each category is described based on their specific distinguishing criteria. These categories can in turn be subdivided into further subcategories based on quality and materials, i.e. on criteria that reflect differences in potential resource consumption during production. The available range of goods in a main category is valuable information for consumers during the annual planning procedure even if they don't have to identify subcategories in their consumption proposals. However, there will in any event of course still be plenty of room for variation and diversity regarding form and design, colour, size, etc. within each subcategory.

In their production proposals worker councils specify for every subcategory of good they plan to produce both the number of units and resource usage. In other words, a worker council's total production cost has to be allocated to the subcategories of goods which they propose to produce.[35] When all consumption and production proposals in an iteration

---

34 That is; a pricing that reflects the social costs for producing the goods. Note that the categorisation of goods and services is not about creating an indefinite number of subcategories which will morph into "brands" for marketing purposes, which is common in today's system, but about creating the best conditions for an efficient and fair planning of production.

35 Most companies do such cost allocations already today in preparation for decisions about pricing of different products and for valuation of their inventory. Product cost

are submitted there is information about excess demand or excess supply for each coarse category of goods, which is the information that the IFB uses when adjusting prices for the next round of proposals. But there is also information about the worker councils' *average production* cost for every coarse category good *AND* for each more detailed subcategory good.

Derived pricing of products in subcategories

Based on information from the aggregated production proposals the worker councils and the industries can calculate a derived unit price for each subcategory of good, even though the IFB only announces prices for main coarse categories. The ratio between the *current Price* (P) and the *Total Average Production Cost* (TAPC) for a unit of a main category product (P/TAPC) indicates a relation which, for our purposes, can be assumed to apply generally to all relevant subcategories. This means that the derived price for a product in a subcategory (p) can be calculated by multiplying the ratio P/TAPC for the main category with any subcategory's average production cost (apc).

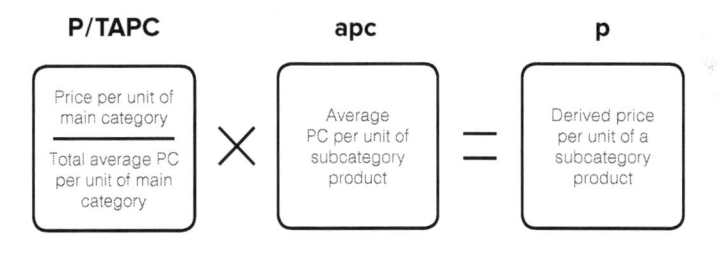

$$\frac{P}{TAPC} \times apc = p$$

$$\frac{\text{Price per unit of main category}}{\text{Total average PC per unit of main category}} \times \text{Average PC per unit of subcategory product} = \text{Derived price per unit of a subcategory product}$$

PC = Production Cost

Figure 5.6. Derived prices of products in sub-categories

This way of deriving prices for subcategory goods makes it possible for worker councils to evaluate their own and other councils' production proposals, and real production during a year, in a more fair and just way since the derived prices take into account that the production of different subcategory products require different quantities and categories of raw

---

calculation is already today an important part of any manufacturing company's internal cost accounting routines.

materials, inputs and other resources, and thus costs society different amounts to produce. Furthermore, a detailed product categorisation enables a more exact charge of production costs to a consumer's account when she picks up products from a distribution centre. The result is a higher degree of fairness and efficiency[36].

When worker councils plan their production for next year they are first and foremost guided by prices and consumers' demand for main category goods. They decide at their own discretion how to allocate their production among different subcategories of goods. In order to guide such production allocation decisions the industry federations may organise shared support units with the task of providing statistics, historical data and forecasts of future trends and distribution of demand between different sub-categories of goods. Such shared support units may also be useful if planning, production and deliveries for other reasons will require elements of coordination and distribution within the industry federations.

Complex products

It may be difficult to standardise and define certain complex products and projects in a way that enables easy and straightforward requests during the annual planning procedure. It could be any type of good or service, final products as well as intermediate and capital goods. It could be custom made final products, or services that need to adapt to changing circumstances which cannot be foreseen before the implementation, and that sometimes even have to be implemented "on a current account". Many projects and tasks in the construction industry are examples of this type of production (e.g. the construction, maintenance and repairs of buildings bridges, sports stadiums, airports, etc.). Such products and projects are ultimately defined by the component products and services, which it is possible to easily define and price, and that together make up the final product. The goal from a planning point of view must in this case be to identify "cost drivers"[37] which can

---

36 In chapter 4 we described how differences between a coarse pricing during the annual planning and a more detailed pricing when the implementing the plan during the year can be handled in the individual consumers' accounts.

37 The term "cost-driver" is today mostly associated with an internal cost accounting model called "Activity Based Costing" (ABC) whose main purpose it is to rationalise a production unit's manufacturing processes. Simply put ABC costing is about esti-

be used to estimate as correctly as possible the resource consumption and costs for different types of activities and projects at an aggregate level in the economy, and to which actors can relate when proposing their production and consumption in the annual planning procedure. A cost driver may be thought of as representing a sort of "basket" with a set of goods and resources that is required for a specific activity or type of project based on aggregated statistics and historical data, or alternatively based on new estimates. During a year, however, each component good and resource is provided separately by the different worker councils. This type of production often requires more planning and coordination between different workplaces during the implementation and may therefore place great demands on effective coordination procedures within and maybe also between industry federations. The worker councils design their own routines for coordination within and between industry federations at their sole discretion and to their best abilities, within the federation structure and potentially other established cooperative bodies.

One important aspect of project production, which actually is important for all production in a participatory economy (and in other types of economies as well) is the question of how to resolve disputes about whether delivered goods fulfil their stipulated quality, or, when it comes to services performed on an ongoing basis, whether the duration of the assignment and performance of the service is acceptable. The definitions of categories of products and services put more or less strict limits on the design and quality of different goods and services. The worker councils are free to design their products and services as they see fit within the limits of the respective subcategory definition. The worker councils are credited only for deliveries that are accepted by the recipients. In cases where differences of opinion occur between the supplier and recipient of a good or service, regarding whether it is up to standard, there needs to be a process in place to handle these disputes including disputes about who should bear the cost of the production of rejected goods and services. In the case of complex projects, a final

---

mating a company's costs for different activities by identifying "cost drivers" for key activities and then trace and map the degree to which other activities and objects consume or use these cost drivers during production. Our use of "cost drivers" in the context above, in contrast, would only be about facilitating the preparation of production proposals in the economy's annual planning procedure.

inspection of the end result by an independent body, where both quality and resource consumption is considered, may be necessary before a project is considered to be approved and completed.[38] Even in the case of deliveries of conventional goods and services, the recipient should have the opportunity to assess the quality and approve or return a delivery. This task may require separate bodies within both consumer and producer federations.

Finally, there is yet another type of good whose treatment in the planning procedure needs mentioning; consumables. Nobody expects a worker council to specify how many packs of paper clips, thumbtacks, pencils or light bulbs it will need for the upcoming year. These type of goods are presumably best dealt with by creating standardised compositions of goods, or "baskets" of goods, with different profiles based on what type of production or activity that is performed, much in the same way as for certain consumer goods which was described in chapter 4 in the section *Individual consumption and the categorisation of goods and services*. The worker councils will in these cases indicate which profile or basket of goods that it has a demand for instead of identifying the demand for each and every item.

Above we have mainly been focusing on the categorisation and definitions of final products since there are crucial differences between producer and consumer demands on the categorisation of these goods that must be managed in a way which both promote efficiency and equity. Categorisation of intermediate goods, goods used in production of final products, should be less of a problem as these goods are both manufactured and used by producers who have similar demands on the categorisation. It may, however, in some cases be advantageous for producers of intermediate goods to work with "baskets" of goods, as well, in the annual planning. Some intermediate goods are specially designed for specific end products, and differ from each other regarding the resource consumption during production, even though they belong to the same main category of goods. In such cases, "baskets" of intermediate goods may enable producers to better meet the overall requested mix of different variants of intermediate goods in the same main category in the annual planning. Many intermediate goods, e.g. various basic commodities, are

---

38   Similar routines for inspections of big projects exist already in today's capitalist system, for example in the construction industry.

easy to categorise, with few variations. It seems reasonable to assume that the categorisation of such inputs therefore is an easier task for the industry federations than the categorisation of consumer end products where consumers' needs of simplicity and flexibility in the annual planning procedure is combined with a desire for variety and diversity in the range of products.

FULFILLING PRODUCTION PLANS

But what suggests that worker councils will prepare and submit production proposals that are based on their actual ability to fulfil their proposals or that the production proposals will consider expected distribution of demand between different subcategories of goods and services? Won't worker councils first and foremost prepare their production proposals in order to get their proposals approved, regardless of actual productive capacity, and regardless of expected distribution of demand between subcategories of goods? In other words, what incentives do worker councils have to prepare and submit production proposals that reflect their actual productive capacity and to consider expected distribution of demand between different subcategories of goods and services?

Note first of all that in a participatory economy, contrary to a centrally planned economy, potentially there could be an incentive for worker councils to *exaggerate* their productive capacity during the annual planning procedure in order to get proposals accepted by other councils and to gain access to productive resources. And in a participatory economy there could be an incentive for worker councils when preparing their proposals to exaggerate production of subcategories of goods that require fewer and cheaper resources, and underestimate the production of subcategories of goods that require more expensive resources compared to the expected demand in order to improve the production proposals SB/SC ratios. How would a participatory economy handle this?

An approved annual plan for the economy means that every worker council has an approved production plan that specify the resources - categories of capital, labour and inputs - that the council will have access to during the year, and the number of main category goods and services that they have committed to produce using the requested resources. Large deviations from the approved plan during the year require approval from the industry federation. There is no reason for other worker councils to approve a production proposal in the annual planning procedure, which obviously overestimates the production capacity or ignores a forecasted demand distribution.

But it is also in an individual worker council's interest to submit a production proposal that it has the potential to fulfil. Firstly, if a worker council fails to produce the amount of goods and services that it has committed to in the annual planning because it overstated its productive potential, or if a worker council fails to dispose of produced goods and services because it did not consider expected demand distribution and/or other worker councils' production, it risks not being able to reach the SB/SC ratio it has committed to in the annual planning procedure, and therefore also risks being assigned fewer consumption points than expected in the coming year, as we described at the beginning of this chapter. Secondly, if a worker council continuously for several years fails to reach its commitments from the annual planning procedure, the industry federation should have the right, after one or two warnings and after offers of help, to forfeit the worker council's membership in the federation since the worker council in such case will have acted in an irresponsible way and wasted society's common resources.

SERVICES

Service production differs in many respects from production of goods. Often, for example in production of health care and education, the service is largely defined in the actual meeting between the service provider and the person receiving it.

Also, service production is typically more labour intensive than the production of goods, and therefore does not provide the same opportunity to reduce costs, for example through technological innovation, development of productive resources or by working faster. It may even have a negative impact on the quality of a service if a worker council producing services tries to minimise labour costs since this can lead to stress, which in turn can lead to more mistakes, carelessness etc.

The provision of health care services and many other services are furthermore strongly associated with specific facilities and buildings (hospitals, schools, cinemas, theatres, sports stadiums, etc.) which consumers in a participatory economy control the design, production and supply of. The production of services in general is usually linked to a limited geographical area, for example, a neighbourhood, a community or region, in a different way than the production of goods. A physical product may, on the other hand, easily be transported anywhere in the entire world.

These circumstances warrant that consumers in some cases, based on the self-management principle, should have a greater influence on the design and organisation of service production as compared to the organisation of commodity production. This suggests in turn that much of a community's service production for end consumers should be organised within the framework of collective consumption as described in the previous chapter. In the end, however, it is the future members of a participatory economy that will decide how to classify and organise the production and consumption of services.

Services produced for end users in the production sector may schematically be divided into two groups. One group contains various administrative services and support functions which in today's economy are produced either (a) internally in shared corporate entities which "sell" their services to other group companies and sometimes also externally to other companies, or (b) in specialised external consultant firms that sell their services externally. It seems reasonable to assume that many of these services will be "internalised" and produced in each workplace in a participatory economy and in this way increase the level of self-management and thus also enhance the feasibility of an equitable division of work tasks. But some support functions and "consulting services" that require expertise and special training will also presumably be organised in specific shared support units. It may be pure R&D units, units that facilitate the implementation of new technology, units providing and analysing industry statistics, units that facilitate accounting, or coordinate major production projects and so on. Discussions and decisions about the creation and organisation of such support units and their funding is presumably best managed in the long-term planning.

The second group of services with end users in the production sector are services that from a planning and categorisation perspective in one way or another are associated with and relate to the produced goods and resources. It may include installation, transportation, operating and maintenance tasks for productive equipment where the categorisation of services can be based on the delivered equipment and on detailed descriptions of what should be included in the service or maintenance commitments.

CHAPTER 6

LONG-TERM PLANNING

So far we have discussed the technical aspects of accounting that primarily are significant for the annual planning and for the ongoing recording of economic activities during a year. In this chapter we will focus on long-term development and investment planning.

Annual planning, investment planning and development planning differ with respect to their time perspective:

Development planning involves decisions that have a major impact on the economy's direction for a long time to come e.g. should we replace fossil fuels with renewable energy and, if so, in what way and how quickly; do we need to organise community infrastructure in our neighbourhoods in a certain way to reduce energy consumption, etc.

Investment planning is based on the decisions in the development planning. It prepares plans for the development of the productive capacities of industries for the next five years and specifies the concrete investments that need to be made in that period and especially in the year to come. The investment plan decides the division between investment and consumption for the upcoming year, and thus creates the conditions for the annual planning procedure. In other words, investment planning makes decisions about the development of society's capital stock, its size and composition for the next five years.

The aim for the procedures regarding long-term economic decision-making is for them to also be based on the values of participatory economics; self-management, justice, efficiency, solidarity, diversity, and ecological sustainability. But to what extent is it possible to organise long-term planning along the lines of the annual planning procedure so that individual worker councils and neighbourhood consumer councils can propose and revise their own activities which are then approved or rejected by other councils over a number of iterations? Long-term planning involves a number of complications that hamper such an approach. The further into the future we try to see, the more uncertainty we face. Technical 'know-how' and people's preferences change over time. Perhaps the most difficult complication is that future opportunity costs and social costs are affected by the investments we decide on today. When we invest in increased productive capacity in an industry, the future opportunity cost of capital assets and social costs of products are affected because the potential supply is changing. The prices for different capital assets, goods and services that the annual planning procedure generates thus become misleading when we make decisions about long-term investments. It is the future opportunity costs and social costs that we need to estimate in order to decide which investments offer the best long-term social return relative to the investment cost. Today's prices provide no reliable guidance in this respect.

These circumstances mean that representatives from industry federations and consumer federations will have to play a greater role in the development and investment planning compared to the annual planning, and be assigned a large part of the responsibility for formulating, reviewing and approving development and investment plans, with the support of workers whose job it is to estimate and explain the possible effects of alternative courses of action. The quantitative estimates of opportunity costs, social costs and social benefits of different investment options and development options in the long term planning will be less reliable than estimates for resources, goods and services in the annual planning. Therefore the actors must be allowed to discuss and debate various alternative scenarios before a limited number of alternative plans may be presented and possibly voted on by all the economy's members. Of course, this does not mean that individual worker councils and consumer councils are excluded from long-term planning, but it does mean that their suggestions and comments more often must go through the elected federation representatives.

INDUSTRIES AND THE CLASSIFICATION OF FEDERATIONS

All worker councils in a participatory economy belong to an industry federation and all industry federations are part of a federation structure with several levels. Federations exist to facilitate economic democracy and self-management, and to facilitate coordination of decisions and activities that affect not only individual worker councils but larger groups of worker councils. The aim for the grouping of worker councils into federations is that federations, as far as possible, should include councils that are affected in a similar manner and to the same extent by the decisions that the federations at different levels make. In order to achieve the greatest possible degree of self-management, when grouping worker councils into industry federations, the worker councils need to consider factors such as: the size of production units, whether the production is capital intensive or labour intensive and requires or is promoted by large production batches or if there exists other economies of scale, and the extent to which the production requires a high degree of coordination between worker councils or if it can be performed relatively independently.

In certain industries, there may exist natural "entry barriers", for example due to economies of scale, which make it difficult for aspiring worker councils to enter the industry. This may potentially lead to monopoly situations which in a capitalistic economy create opportunities to reap extra high profits, but in a participatory economy manifest itself as possibilities for workers in these industries to lower their efforts without receiving lower work compensation.

The federations play an important role in the development planning and investment planning. Furthermore, it could be decided that it is the other members in the industry federation that approve or reject an individual worker council's production proposal in the annual planning procedure. The federations may in this context need to establish special committees for reviewing proposals that do not reach an approved SB/SC ratio, when there is reason to believe that the numbers do not tell the whole story or in situations when exemptions from the SB/SC ratio requirement could be justified.

Members in industry federations also decide on individual worker councils' admissions and exclusions to and from federations. When a worker council applies for admission to a federation, the federation needs to assess the council's credibility and its ability to fulfilling its production proposals. It may in this context be relevant to decide, for example, on a criterion for the number of approved members that an aspiring worker council must be able to show relative to its total need for labour according to its production proposal. When the industry federation accepts a worker council as a member it functions as a kind of licensor that entitles the council to apply for access to a start-up set of productive assets and then participate in the annual planning procedure by preparing and submitting production proposals. The existing members of an industry federation may have an incentive to restrict the number of new entrants in order to limit the total output of the industry's products or services, the prices of which would thus be higher, making it easier for existing members to reach a SB/SC ratio exceeding 1. It may therefore be necessary to establish procedures allowing aspiring members to challenge industry federations on their decision of refusal of entry, and take it to a "higher" level where several industries are represented.

Worker councils that fail to submit a proposal that is approved by the other worker councils in the annual planning, or repeatedly fail to live up to their obligations from the annual planning, or otherwise behave irresponsibly may after one or more warnings be deemed to have exhausted their membership in the federation and be excluded. The productive resources that are thereby released will be available in the remaining iterations in the annual planning procedure, or, if there are resources, the use of which require longer foresight in the next annual planning. Larger plants and facilities that are released in this way may need to be adapted to new areas of use before being made available again.

Industry federations and their representatives also have a prominent role in case an annual plan needs to be renegotiated or adjusted during a year due to changed circumstances. Adjustments of an annual plan need to be negotiated by industry federations, together with representatives from consumer federations. Finally, industry federations have a responsibility to make sure that the goods and services that worker councils produce hold a comparable standard and that the goods produced reach the criteria that the industry has set. For example, light bulbs that are manufactured by worker councils need to meet standards relating to size, quality, electrical current, performance, etc., that are set by the electrical industry.

The classification and design of industries is obviously something that a future participatory economy will decide on its own but to illustrate the task, we will here sketch a possible industry classification of worker councils. At the most general level an economy's worker councils could be divided into a few main federations according to the general function they perform in the economy, such as (1) agriculture, forestry and fishing (2) extraction of minerals (3) manufacturing (4) construction (5) freight and transport. Each of these main federations could then be divided into sub federations in one or more levels based on a more detailed breakdown of the groups of goods and services that the worker councils produce. Worker councils that produce components to final products may form their own sub federations under the federation defined by the final products, while worker councils that produce intermediate products used more widely in many different final products may form separate federations. The lowest sub federations, finally, may be divided into groups that separate different production technologies within federations.

If some worker councils predominantly produce for deliveries to consumer federations in a limited geographical area, or if it is practical, or if for any other reason it increases the degree of self-management or justice, the above described federation division may be supplemented by a geographical division. In any event, the goal of the formation of federations and industry classification is to create the best possible conditions for self-management, and for efficient and equitable decisions during the annual planning, long-term planning and when implementing the plans.

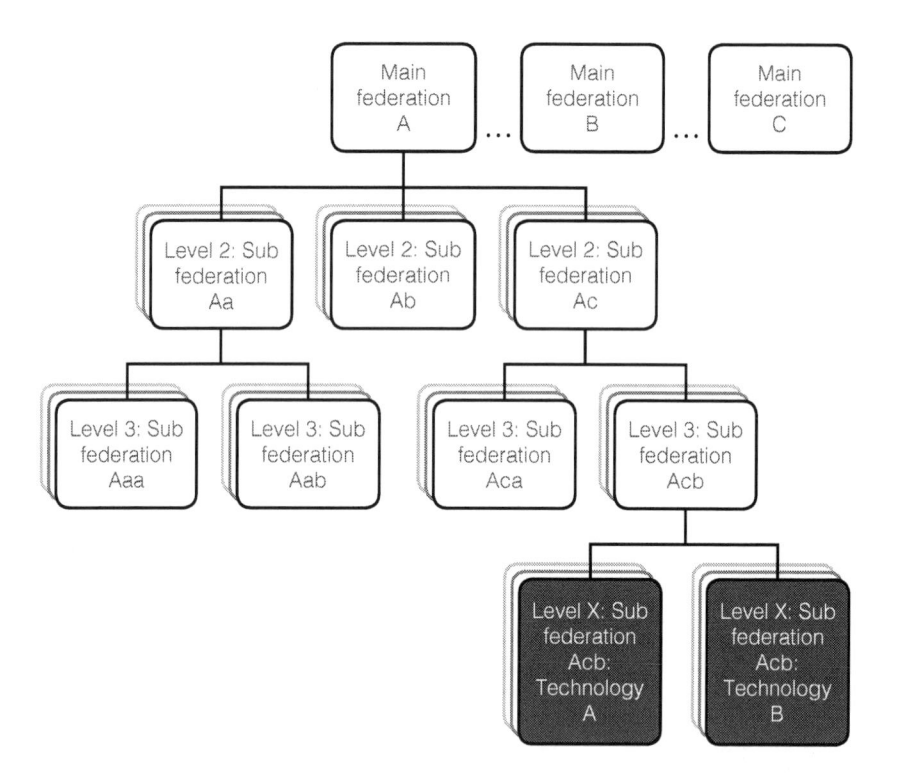

Figure 6.1. Industry Federation Structure

SOCIETY'S PRODUCTIVE CAPACITY

In the previous chapter, we discussed the allocation of *user rights* that give access to existing productive resources. In this section we focus instead on the planning and decisions regarding the development of society's productive capacity, i.e. which productive resources should be produced and in what quantity, and how they should be distributed between different *industries*. Investment planning is based on the development planning and enable the implementation of the long term development projects that the economy has decided. The accounting implications of the implementation of an agreed on investment plan were described in chapter 3 under the section "Society's investment fund".

PRODUCTIVE CAPITAL

To all intents and purposes, the economy's available productive resources, production technologies and customer preferences are fixed and given when the annual planning procedure starts. It is this that makes it possible to estimate the opportunity costs and social costs with some accuracy during the annual planning iterations. Society's total productive capacity is known and specified by industry, technology, right down to capital category. In the investment planning procedure representatives from industry federations and consumer federations together with various specialists propose, discuss and plan the detailed composition of the economy's available stock of productive resources for the upcoming years.

In order to do this effectively without wasting scarce resources, the representatives need to get an idea of the Social Rate of Return on Investment - SROI - for different investment options, which is the social benefits that the investments are expected to generate in relation to their social costs. As we noted above, this is associated with considerable uncertainty since, among other things, the future opportunity costs and social costs that we need to estimate and assess are affected by the investments that the decisions are all about. The accounting system can in principle only provide information about SROI for historical investments, which at best can provide a rough indication and a starting point for further discussion regarding future investments.

A crucial issue that the investment planning participants must consider and decide at an early stage of the planning process is the distribution between consumption and investments for the upcoming years. Society's productive capacity cannot increase unless part of the available productive resources in a given year is used for the production of capital goods instead of consumer goods. In other words, the economy needs to decide on a trade-off between greater consumption today (less investments today) and greater consumption in the future (more investment today). Put simply, the community needs to decide how much it wants to "save" rather than consume. The higher the rate of investment, the fewer consumer goods can be produced.

During the development and investment planning the economy has to assess which *industries* can be expected to create the greatest social benefit in relation to investment costs - SROI - and how large capacity increases would be justified, and which industries are not expected to create a positive SROI and in which case the production capacity may even need to be reduced. In this context the industry federations need to consider a variety of factors that are more or less difficult to assess, in addition to the problem of circular dependency described above, such as expected levels of technological innovation and development in different industries. They need to discuss preferred industry structure in terms of geographical spread, unit size and different production technologies, and they need to consider potential economies of scale for different technologies. They have to decide how quickly they want to implement structural changes and changes in production technologies. Furthermore, they need to assess whether a planned increase in production capacity should be achieved through more and new production units or through additional investments in existing units, or through a combination of both. And similarly they need to decide if a planned capacity reduction should be achieved through closure of production units or an adjustment of existing units' capacities or a combination of both.[39] All these decisions and circumstances affect which capital categories to produce.

Furthermore, they need to consider the age of the existing capital stocks in different industries and estimate how much of the different categories of capital will be fully depreciated during the year and therefore need to be replaced. In other words, they need to assess the need for replacement investment. The total investment requirement for each category of capital can schematically be defined as:

Investment requirement in a period = Total capital needed to reach the desired productive capacity – Initial capital stocks + Consumption of existing capital during the period.

---

39   In certain circumstances society might want to implement a necessary structural change of productive capacity in a slower pace than is economically justified.

The investment planning procedure should result in a detailed statement of goals for the development of productive capacity for each industry for the next few years, specified per category of capital and geographic distribution regarding fixed facilities, including a description of the investment requirements per category of capital for the upcoming year.

All assessments and estimates about future development, and all other assumptions that the federations make when they decide on future investments and development projects under the long-term planning procedure, are communicated to all actors and anchored at the level of the individual councils. All decisions are public and available to all actors prior to the annual planning procedure. After a well performed, transparent and democratic long-term planning process it is expected that there exists a consensus among the worker councils, federations and expert advisors regarding the forecasts of future developments. But individual worker councils may of course have dissenting views and establish their production proposals during the annual planning procedure based on them.

When it comes to the planning of society's development of new and existing natural capital, society, for the sake of ecological sustainability and intergenerational equity, needs to consider how the decisions will affect the future generations' possibilities for a good life and their well-being, including their access to a prospering natural environment. Society needs to take into account that certain natural resources and ecosystems are irreplaceable and may have a great value in and of themselves, regardless of the extent to which they are productive in an economic sense, and that there are threshold effects that at all costs must be avoided in order not to trigger irreversible feedback loops with potentially disastrous effects on the environment. The precautionary principle should be applied when there is uncertainty about the negative effects of excessive exploitation of a particular natural resource.

SHARED SUPPORT UNITS

A participatory economy may establish different types of shared support units at various levels in the economy in order to efficiently handle tasks that the whole economy, or all worker councils in an industry federation or in a group of federations benefit from. Examples of shared support units include, Research & Development (R&D) units, units that facilitate decisions, coordination and implementation of plans and activities, etc. Perhaps the most prominent support unit is the Iteration Facilitation Board. Support units are self-managed worker councils that are responsible to serving either the economy as a whole or individual industry federations and have no influence over decisions besides decisions about their own internal work organisation. They are appointed and dissolved based on the economy's or the federations' assessments of the social benefit that they add. The economy, or the industry federations, may put restrictions on the time for job assignments in support units if long assignments will lead to undue opportunities to influence other workers or if there is a risk for concentration of power. The support units fulfil tasks that potentially have a major impact on society's and the industries' present and future productive capacity. We look at three such tasks below; (a) research and development (b) decision and coordination support to worker councils and industry federations, and (c) the implementation of investment decisions.

Research and development

Research and development (R&D) is a collective "good" that advantageously can be discussed and planned during the investment planning and the long term development planning. This applies both to the development of new products, production technology and organisation of work. R&D often requires considerable resources. Any potential positive results are often realised in a more or less distant future and there is no guarantee that research efforts will generate positive results. R&D units may be subordinate to individual industry federations, while the allocation of funds is discussed and decided collectively by all federations during the investment planning. A special version of R&D efforts are activities undertaken to determine if natural capital resources will contain assets that can be extracted in an efficient way without harming the environment too much and therefore justifies investment.

Decision and coordination support

The worker councils and industry federations need to consider many options and make many decisions during the long-term planning, the annual planning, when implementing the plans, and in potential negotiations regarding adjustments of an agreed on annual plan. In order for decisions to be fair and efficient, the information on which decisions are based needs to be as extensive, accurate and precise as the circumstances permit, which may mean that there should be a set of worker councils whose job it is to create and provide both qualitative and quantitative information to the actors. The work tasks could involve presenting historical data, assessing the probabilities of alternative scenarios, in different ways coordinate and facilitate the implementation of decisions, etc. These worker councils could be organised in networks of shared administrative support units which are linked to the various industry federations and whose tasks are defined during the long-term planning. Workers in such administrative support units are responsible for generating useful information in order to support decision making and have no actual influence over decisions.

Implementation of investment decisions

The investment planning procedure culminates in a relatively detailed description of the objectives for the production and scrapping of productive capital, including maintenance in some cases and replacement and supplementary investments, and the implementation of other projects in the next years specified by industry and capital categories. But who is responsible for the implementation of the investment plans? Someone must make concrete proposals and ask for the production (and possibly maintenance) of capital goods in the annual planning procedure, and facilitate the implementation of the decisions during the year. There is thus a need for separate units for the administration of capital assets for each industry - special worker councils - which convert investment decisions into proposals in the annual planning procedure, and initiate discussions regarding adjustments of investment plans if indicative prices and/or other circumstances change dramatically during the annual planning iterations, and implement and monitor proposals that are approved in the annual plan and compare them with the original investment plan. These administration units for capital assets may also function as kind of "brokers" during the year, who will facilitate transfers of capital assets between worker councils. They may also be assigned the responsibility to compile information about the supply of capital assets based on decisions made in the investment planning procedure and the demand that emerges during the annual planning.

The fact that society's demand for newly produced capital goods is known from the investment planning procedure when the annual planning starts may pose a problem. It presents an opportunity for the worker councils producing capital goods to use this knowledge for their own gain at the expense of society by restricting their proposals for production of capital goods, thus driving up prices. This is a general problem that exists in all types of economies when a small number of producers have knowledge of the demand curve for the products they produce, whether they form a formal cartel or not.[40] Such attempts to manipulate prices need to be monitored and discouraged by the economy, perhaps by the IFB which may be instructed to hold back price adjustments upwards if such behaviour is identified.

The funding of support units

The accounting of transfers of funds to support units is described in chapter 3. What separates a support unit from an ordinary worker council, with regard to accounting and funding, is that a support unit is not credited any social benefit for its deliveries of services at the time of delivery. Instead it receives funds - a budget – based on decisions by society or by industry federations, in return for the provision of a specific shared support function that is available to all worker councils in one or more industry federations or in the whole economy, during a certain period of time.

LABOUR

A society's supply of labour and its "quality" in terms of education, technical "know-how", experience, etc. is of great importance for society's productive capacity. This is also sometimes called society's "human capital", and it can be shaped and adapted in different ways. By providing and designing basic education and vocational training, society affects the workforce characteristics and composition in a very concrete way. A participatory economy will place different requirements on the workforce's skills compared to today's capitalist system. For example, workplaces are expected to balance jobs with respect to empowering tasks, and to the extent possible also with respect to desirability, which requires comprehensive training - although specialisation of course will be necessary and desirable. The number of vocational training places in society and their orientations, and hence the design of the future labour

---

40 Dominating corporation constellations that influence and even control price setting is a problem in many capitalist market economies, where large company mergers have been very common the last thirty years.

supply, should presumably be discussed among the worker councils' representatives in the industry federations during the long-term development planning and investment planning, and be adapted in light of the planned capacity development in different industries as well as to the requirements imposed by the jobs' design and balancing.

Furthermore, through their federations the worker councils need to discuss, decide and continuously monitor how the classification of labour into different labour categories shall be determined and defined. The categorisation of labour needs to consider both function and experience as well as the requirements of job balancing with regard to versatility and society's need for specialisation. Labour categorisation both influences and is influenced by society's educational and training programs and worker councils' organisation of work and production.

Some necessary tasks in a society will inevitably be less desirable and less pleasant to perform than others, and while workers in the economy may seek to fairly distribute these tasks between themselves, it may, after best attempts, prove to be unfeasible to do with any high degree of accuracy. If one worked hour is compensated with the same number of consumption points regardless of the work task's level of desirability, the labour categories that include unpleasant but necessary tasks will have a constant excess demand.

In order to increase the supply of labour categories that perform necessary but unpleasant and less desirable tasks, the compensation for performing such work tasks may need to be adjusted upwards. The adjustments may be calculated and expressed as a percentage of the basic compensation per worked hour in the economy. The total sum of all adjustments for all work tasks in the economy should come to zero, i.e. the average compensation per worked hour in the economy should not be affected by these adjustments, which means that work tasks with a higher desirability on average will have to be compensated with fewer consumption points per worked hour. These adjustments are carried out, and affect the amount of consumption points that an individual *workplace* is allocated for internal distribution, *independently* of the allotment of consumption points that is based on effort and that was described in chapter 5.

Adjustments for differences in desirability of work tasks are about increasing the supply of labour categories for which demand cannot be reduced further for example by investing in technology to replace the unpleasant tasks. The task of adjusting compensation for differences in desirability between work tasks is presumably best handled before the annual planning procedure, in the long-term planning where the supply of labour and the industries' capacity development is planned.

Finally, a participatory economy can and should establish shared support units with the task of assisting workers that are looking for a new job or a new worker council, if they don't thrive, or if they want to move to a new neighbourhood. Such "employment service units" are of great importance both for the workers' personal freedom of choice, and the labour supply's flexibility.

TRADE WITH OTHER ECONOMIES

When there are big differences in opportunity costs for production of goods between different regions and economies, there are also potential efficiency gains to be achieved by specialisation of production and trade, even though these benefits sometimes are exaggerated. For a participatory economy the goal must be to negotiate terms of trade with other economies that are consistent with the fundamental values of participatory economics - justice, self-management, solidarity, diversity, efficiency and ecological sustainability - regardless of whether the trading partners are functional participatory economies or capitalist economies.

If a participatory economy is trading with a relatively richer economy it should aim to obtain as large part as possible of the efficiency gain resulting from the trade and certainly not below 50%. If a participatory economy, on the other hand, is trading with a relatively poorer economy it should accept to receive less than 50 percent of the efficiency gain, and be content to see its poorer trading partner receive the majority of the gain. If efficiency gains from trade is distributed in this way it gradually reduces the gap between richer and poorer trading partners. Note that this rule for allocation of efficiency gains from trade applies regardless of whether the trading partner is a participatory economy or a capitalist economy. Citizens in a poorer economy on average receive a lower compensation for their efforts than citizens in richer economies, and by using the "50 percent" rule when trading, a participatory economy confirms that "justice" means that the same effort or sacrifice should be compensated to the same degree. A participatory economy cannot argue that the principle of justice is not applicable to trade with capitalist economies, on grounds that the citizens of such an economy may not necessarily support the same principle of justice. The point is that its values preclude a participatory economy from interacting with other economies on conditions which it *itself* considers to be unfair.[41]

When a participatory economy is forming its trade policy it needs to consider many factors. The decisions regarding trade policy both affect and are affected by other long-term planning decisions. The effects of imports on domestic production and consumption need to be analysed. Perhaps there are goods that the economy for one reason or another regards as so harmful that importing them altogether should not be allowed, for example goods that affect the environment or health negatively. Imports of both capital goods and consumer goods have effects on the development of domestic production that need to be analysed and assessed. Maybe society wants to protect a certain domestic production during a construction phase by temporarily restricting imports. Similarly, the export of goods have effects on the economies receiving the goods that need to be analysed based on a participatory economy's values. In general terms, exports are justified if the resulting social benefit is greater than the benefit that would have resulted from domestic consumption, and imports are justified if the social costs will be lower than they would have been by domestic production.

If an economy's exports exceed its imports it means that the economy is saving i.e. that the consumers collectively are not using all their consumption points and/or that the investment fund is not using all its investment capacity. If an economy's imports instead exceeds its exports it means that the consumer collective and/or the investment fund are incurring debt at an aggregated level. Funds that an economy receives as a result of transactions with external economies can by necessity only be used for other transactions that generate outflows, and outflows of funds from an economy has to be met by other transactions that generate inflows. If an economy's import is larger than its export, the economy must borrow from external economies (or decrease its currency reserve). If an economy's export is larger than its import, the economy must buy assets (or invest) in external economies (or increase its currency reserve). A participatory economy needs to consider to what degree it wants to participate in such

---

41 For a more detailed discussion about the 50% rule and about a Participatory Economy's participation in the global economy see Robin Hahnel. *Economic Justice and Democracy: From Competition to Cooperation*, Routledge Books 2005 pages 207-213

financial transactions with external economies. If, for whatever reason, it doesn't want to borrow funds from or invest funds in external economies, its total size of imported goods and services need to be matched by an equivalent size of exports, which naturally limits the "freedom of action" with regard to trade and transactions with other economies.

BALANCE OF PAYMENTS WITH OTHER ECONOMIES

Exports − imports of goods and services +/− investments, transfers and other payments

---

Figure 6.2. Society's balance of payments

It is the economy, in the form of representatives from industry federations and consumer federations, which negotiate and establish the objectives and guidelines for trade with other economies in preparation for the annual planning procedure, and thus, in principle, plan and control the "supply" of imported goods and the economy's "demand" for exported goods. During the annual planning procedure the economy needs to be represented by, for example an "acting committee for trade with other economies," or similar which "converts" the decisions in the long-term planning procedures into proposals of export and import of various categories of goods in response to worker councils' proposals for their exports and imports. The economy's "internal" prices of imported and exported goods in the annual planning procedure are then determined in the same way as prices for domestically produced and consumed goods, and may therefore not necessarily correspond to the prices that the economy pays, and is paid, by its external trading partners. In fact, the indicative prices of imported and exported goods in the annual planning procedure may start with the expected "real" prices that will be paid to and received from external trading partners, to which the IFB then adds mark-ups and mark-downs, in light of supply and demand, with the aim to reach the established goals for the external trade.

EXPORT AND IMPORT BY WORKER COUNCILS

When a worker council in a participatory economy exports or imports goods to/from a company in an external economy, it is *society* or the economy that for accounting purposes represents the worker council's counterpart, not the company in the external country that ships or receives the goods. Otherwise all transactions are registered in the same way as for domestic purchases and deliveries based on the prices that are decided during the annual planning procedure.

Since society is both a worker council's counterpart when international trade takes place, and the entity that receives a surplus from or covers a deficit in a workplace after a year-end, an export or import transaction will not directly affect a worker council's balance with society. A worker council's credit entry for an export transaction, and charge for an import transaction, will affect the surplus (or deficit) that is settled with society at the end of the year, with the exact same amount that affects available funds both in the worker council's and society's accounts in their function as trade partners. The transactions that affect a worker council's balance with society will thus cancel one and other out.

PRICE DIFFERENCES IN INTERNATIONAL TRADE

The "internal" prices for exported and imported goods, which in a participatory economy are decided in the annual planning procedure, and that are guaranteed by society during the year and charged and credited worker councils, need not correspond to the actual prices that are paid to, or received by, external trade partners, since these prices are set on an international market. Price differences may thus arise when trading internationally.

Positive price differences

When the paid prices for imported goods during the year fall below the prices established in the annual planning procedure that worker councils are charged, or when the received prices for exported goods during the year exceeds the established prices that worker councils are credited, there are positive price differences. These price differences will affect the investment fund in the following way:

Available funds is debited and balanced investment funds is credited.

POSITIVE PRICE DIFFERENCE – INTERNATIONAL TRADE	
Dr	Cr
1.) Available funds	2.) Balanced investment funds

Negative price differences

When the paid prices for imported goods during the year exceed the prices established in the annual planning procedure that worker councils are charged, or when the received prices for exported goods during the year fall below the established prices that worker councils are credited, there are negative price differences. These price differences will affect the investment fund in the following way:

NEGATIVE PRICE DIFFERENCE – INTERNATIONAL TRADE	
Dr	Cr
2.) Balanced investment funds	1.) Available funds

Long-term Planning   141

FUNDS - BALANCES	
Dr	Cr
1.) Available funds	2.) Balanced investment funds
SETTLEMENTS FROM OTHER ENTITIES AND INVESTMENTS	
Dr	Cr
4.) Investments and shared resources - industry federations	3.) Settlements from other entities
a) Productive capital	a) Worker councils
b) Support units	b) Manufactured capital - Industry federations
c) Research and development	c) Natural capital - Industry federations
d) Training and education	5.b) Period end - overspent funds
e) Other investments	
5.a) Period end - unused funds	

Figure 6.3 Society's investment fund

CHAPTER 7

THE ENVIRONMENT

In market economies buyers and sellers have a strong incentive to transfer costs for their own production and consumption to external third parties in society, including costs in terms of any negative environmental impact. This way, buyers and sellers can maximise their profits and promote their own interests at society's expense. The individuals who suffer from these "externalised" costs are usually easy targets since they are both geographically and chronologically scattered, and the negative impact each individual experiences is small and often different from individual to individual. Each individual has thus little incentive to demand influence over the transactions, even if the total sum of all individuals' interests often is considerably greater than the interests of the individual buyers and sellers.[42]

In a participatory economy the polluters are charged for the damage that their pollution creates and those who are affected are compensated for the damage they suffer.[43] Before each iteration round during the annual planning procedure the IFB announces a current cost estimate of the harmful effects that the emission of one unit of each pollutant creates. Worker councils whose production emits pollutants, and Communities of Affected Parties (explained below) react to this cost information. Worker councils which pollute suggest, through their production proposals, how much of each pollutant they plan to discharge, knowing that they will be charged an amount equal to the current cost estimate per unit of the pollutant times the number of units they want to discharge. The harmful effects that their pollution creates thus become part of the worker council's production costs.

Those who are adversely affected by environmentally harmful substances do not necessarily correspond with the residents within the geographical boundaries of consumer councils and federations. There is therefore a need to establish separate communities of affected parties (CAPs) for pollutants with different effects, which bring together all the parties adversely affected by the substance in question, regardless of which consumer council they belong to. These CAPs suggest how many

---

42　In *Green Economics: Confronting the Ecological Crises* Pluto Press 2011, R. Hahnel discusses threats to our environment and what we can do about them today in anticipation of a system change.

43　This chapter is based on Robin Hahnel's descriptions of how the environment would be protected in a participatory economy, for example in *Of the People, By the People: The case for a Participatory Economy*, Soapbox press, 2012.

units of each emission substance that they are willing to allow considering that they will be compensated by an amount equal to the current cost estimate per unit and substance times the number of units that the CAP allows. Society as a whole or any individual CAP may decide that it does not want to allow any emissions at all of a specific substance but if a CAP accepts a certain amount of release it will obtain consumption points as compensation for the damage its members suffer at the current level of emissions. The compensation that members of a CAP receive for exposing themselves to the effects of pollution is added to the compensation that they receive in their workplaces.

The IFB adjusts the indicative cost of damage per unit of different pollution substances based on the difference between the CAPs' proposed amount of emission they will accept, and the worker councils planned quantity of emissions according to their production proposals. This way emission levels will end up at an "efficient" level, in the sense that further releases will be authorised only if the positive social effects of the increased production that results exceed the damaging effects that the affected parties are experiencing. It is no longer possible for individual producers and consumers to shift the costs of environmentally harmful emissions to society.

The way that the annual planning procedure manages pollution as described above protects the environment, but only to the extent that it is the present members of a CAP that are affected by the negative impacts of emissions. Often negative effects of environmentally harmful emissions are very long lasting and persistent, and affects both current residents and future generations negatively. The future generations' interests can only be considered in the long-term development planning by the present generation taking into account the interests of future generations and deciding to limit and adapt their own preferences in light of these considerations during their deliberations on the long-term plans for production and investments. Major and long term changes in the energy, transport and housing sectors are all discussed and adopted during the development planning.

It is the members of a CAP that decide which substances they want to classify as harmful pollutants, the emission levels and pricing of which should be decided in the annual planning procedure. To help decide this, they need the support of R&D units consisting of specialists and researchers who investigate the effects on the environment and climate etc. of different pollutant substances, and how the harmful effects change at different levels of emissions. These R&D units which are subordinate to the various CAPs could be funded through the framework of the collective consumption planning on an overall federation level, as described in Chapter 4. Alternatively, it may be decided that a portion of the compensation that a CAP receives from the polluting worker councils will (co-)finance these R&D units before the remainder of the payment is distributed to the CAP members.

Since membership in a CAP means that a consumer will be entitled to additional compensation, there are strong incentives for individuals to apply for membership and falsely claim that they are negatively affected by certain pollution. Therefore it is unrealistic to leave it to the individuals themselves to determine if they are affected or not, and whether or not they will be granted membership in a CAP. It may be very difficult and time consuming to determine whether an individual is affected by an environmentally harmful substance, and therefore eligible for inclusion in a CAP; however, there is no shortcut to avoid this work. The economy and the individual CAPs must create clear procedures to evaluate and assess each application for membership. Scientific and medical evidence about the effects of various substances may need to be collected, and those whose status as "affected parties" is already decided should have an opportunity to question the legitimacy of new applications. This network of process organisations is another group of support units that need to be established and funded collectively.

Finally, the compensation in the form of consumption points flowing into a CAP from worker councils that emit pollutants can be distributed to CAP members in different ways. It could be used for any form of collective consumption among the CAP's members. Or it could be evenly distributed to all members in the form of equally sized allotments of consumption points that increase their opportunity to consumption during the annual planning. In these cases there are no incentives for existing CAP members to exaggerate the damage they are afflicted. But if a CAP wants to allocate more consumption points to members who are assumed to have suffered greater damage, there arises an opportunity for individuals to take advantage of this by exaggerating their damages. However, today there are several ways to deal with this problem in case a CAP wants to allocate compensation to its members based on the level of damage suffered.

Under the framework described above, in order for the managing of emissions of environmentally harmful pollutants to be effective and fair, the economy as a whole has to be reasonably egalitarian - which a participatory economy would be. If there would exist big differences in wealth and income between groups of affected parties, the poorer groups would be more likely to tolerate higher emissions than the rich groups in order to gain access to more consumption points even though the group's preferences for a healthy environment would be identical. A participatory economy also has several other components which have positive impacts on the environment, for example, it is likely that citizens would choose a much higher level of collective consumption since there is no bias in favour of individual consumption , and collective consumption is less harmful for the environment than individual consumption. And finally, since there is no intrinsic growth imperative in a participatory economy (that is inherent in a market economy), it is reasonable to assume that citizens in a participatory economy would choose shorter working hours, resulting in less production/consumption and a reduction of the impact from economic activity on the environment.

CHAPTER 8

SUMMARY

Any economy has to organise society's production and consumption, facilitate economic decision-making, and allocate both the benefits and burdens resulting from economic cooperation among its population. In order to fulfil these tasks, an economy needs to establish a number of institutions, which simply are sets of interrelated roles that define the actors' expected behaviour in different situations. For example, *the market* is a defining institution of a capitalist economy which, consists of two roles - "buyers" and "sellers" - that members of the economy can assume and whose activities form patterns of expected behaviour. While fulfilling the above mentioned functions, in order to evaluate the performance of an economy and its institutions, we need to have an idea of what our goals are and what values we want the economy to promote.[44]

A participatory economy is defined by four institutions; (1) self-managed worker and consumer councils and their federations, (2) balanced jobs, (3) compensation based on effort and need, and (4) a democratic allocation model that is called participatory planning. These institutions are designed to promote six fundamental values or goals; economic democracy, economic justice, efficiency, solidarity, diversity, and ecological sustainability. Such an economy differs from a capitalist or a market socialist economy in several important respects and the information that a participatory economy's accounting model needs to provide is therefore very different.

In a participatory economy, there are no private equity owners or shareholders who own factories and other production facilities, and who control what is produced and how it is produced, and who strive for maximum personal return on private investment without considering any negative effects on others in society. Goods and services are not traded in a market where individual buyers and sellers try to maximise their own profits at the expense of others in society. Nor are there any private banks or other lenders who control access to credit and thus control investment opportunities for all those who do not have access to private assets. There are no groups of workers whose sole duty is to obey orders or to exclusively perform monotonous tasks, while other workers make all the decisions and monopolise empowering tasks and

---

44 For an excellent introduction to economics (Political Economy) and various tools to analyse and evaluate economies see Hahnel. *The ABCs of Political Economy: A Modern Approach*, Pluto Press, 2014.

access to information. And there are no workers who receive hundreds of times more income than other workers. Any differences in compensation are relatively small and based solely on differences in effort or sacrifice.

In a participatory economy those who are affected by the decisions have influence over them to the extent that they are affected. Consumers propose and adjust their consumption - both private and public - through their consumer councils and federations, and ensure that other consumers' proposed consumption is fair, i.e. whether it is proportionate to their effort and sacrifice. Producers propose and adjust their production through their worker councils and industry federations, and decide whether other worker councils' proposed production is efficient, i.e. that the produced social benefit exceeds the social cost. Representatives of both consumers and producers plan the long term development of the economy and decide on investments in future productive capacity. Society's productive resources in the form of produced and natural capital belong to everyone in society. In order to obtain access to use these commonly owned resources, producers have to demonstrate that they will use them in an efficient and socially responsible way.

For consumers and workers to be able to make all these decisions in a fair and efficient manner, the accounting system has to be designed in a different way than today, and provide different information and economic indicators. For producers to be able to assess whether their own and others' production proposals are efficient and socially responsible, costs and benefits for various economic activities have to reflect *social costs* and benefits of activities, and not as today the individual buyers and sellers' costs and benefits. The cost of using society's productive resources must reflect true opportunity costs, which is the alternative social benefit "sacrificed" or foregone when a productive resource is used in a particular production. Consumers must have access to information that enables them to assess their own and others' efforts in proportion to the social costs of their proposed consumption. And when society is planning future investments in production capacity, the potential social rate of return must be prioritised, and not private investors and lenders potential to maximise profit.

We have in this book outlined an accounting model that meets a participatory economy's information demands. We have identified the main accounting entities, and how different economic transactions can be monitored and recorded in a way that gives actors in the economy access to information that create the best possible conditions for democratic, fair and effective decisions. Decision makers in the economy need to be able to quickly form an opinion on the economic impact of different economic activities, projects and investments, and who will ultimately be burdened with costs and who will enjoy the benefits. An important and prominent aspect has been to discuss the classification of goods, services, labour and productive resources for accounting purposes - on what grounds it should be done - in order for the annual planning procedure to result in prices that reflect social costs and opportunity costs as accurately as possible. In this context, we have proposed accounting solutions to issues relating specifically to the planning, monitoring and accounting of economic activities in a participatory economy, for example:

1. The fees that the individual worker councils are charged for the use of different categories of labour is not correlated, as in a capitalist or socialist market economy, to the income that individual workers receive. The fees for getting access to different labour categories reflect the labour's opportunity cost and is determined by supply and demand during the annual planning procedure, while members' compensations instead are based on their effort and sacrifice.

2. Consumers and producers have different needs and requirements for how the categorisation of goods and services should look like. Consumers want a few coarse categories with as few details as possible when preparing their consumption proposals during the annual planning procedure. Producers, on the other hand, need to consider potential differences in resource usage for production of different versions of goods and services when preparing their production proposals and therefore need to work with more detailed information.

3. The cost that worker councils are charged for access to society's productive capital - the fees for user rights to various categories of capital - are not, as in capitalist market economies, the same as the capital acquisition cost (or depreciation thereof). In a participatory economy the worker councils do not own productive capital, it belongs to all citizens in society. The user right fees that are charged to worker councils for their access to different categories of capital reflect the opportunity cost for the resource and are determined by

supply and demand during the annual planning procedure, while the decisions to produce productive capital (and thus determine the supply) are handled in the investment planning procedure by representatives of consumers and producers and are based on estimates of social return of investment.

4. The costs of harmful effects on the environment caused by producer and consumer activities are not borne, as in capitalist and market socialist economies, by a third party - the community - but by those who cause them. And those who suffer from the adverse effects are compensated. The size of the costs of harmful effects and of the compensation that the affected parties will receive are determined during the iterations in the annual planning procedure.

The implementation of a new accounting system is of course not a task that has, or should have, a high priority in a situation where the daily resistance to the capitalist system is mainly focused on mitigating its worst effects. However, in a situation when we can start to build alternative institutions such as self-managing workplaces, or consumer associations, or participatory budgeting procedures for parts of our collective consumption, visions and ideas about how we can collect, sort and present economic information in order to promote democratic decision making and economic cooperation can have a positive and favourable effect on the development of these institutions. In any case, the future accounting system in the sense of society's overall accounting principles will likely continuously change and evolve, and reflect but also affect the development of economic key institutions such as the ownership of productive resources, allocation systems, compensation models and division of work tasks.

By attempting to provide concrete solutions to real world problems, our aim with this book is to help convey a feeling that alternative non-capitalist economic systems are possible and that alternative visions don't need to be lofty utopias that only dreaming unrealistic romantics are interested in. Most importantly, we hope to inspire and encourage further constructive discussions about how economic visions guided by the values of democracy, justice and sustainability can be implemented on a practical level.

APPENDIX 1:
ACCOUNTING PRIMER

Accounting is about keeping notes of *economic transactions* in order to be able to account for *assets* (cash, receivables, inventory, equipment, machines etc.) and *liabilities* (payables, bank loans, etc.) at a certain time, or *incomes* and *costs* during a certain period. An economic transaction may include a sale or a purchase of a product or a machine, taking out a loan from a bank, or making a payment on a debt.

One usually distinguishes between single and double entry bookkeeping. *Single entry bookkeeping* means that a business transaction is registered only once in one account based on what the transaction refers to. *Double entry bookkeeping* means that a transaction is recorded twice on two different accounts. By using double-entry bookkeeping it is possible to identify both a transaction's effect on the financial position, for instance an increase in assets and at the same time identify *the cause* behind a change, for instance increased revenues or a decrease in another asset.

Economic transactions are recorded in a number of different *accounts* which specify what the transaction refers to in more detail. Each account has two sides, a left side called *debit (Dr)* and a right side called *credit (Cr)*. In double-entry bookkeeping the sum of all registrations in debit must always equal the sum of all registrations in credit, both for every individual entry and totally for all entries i.e. the accounting transactions must balance.

Example of a transaction entry

CASH (ASSETS)		
Dr	Cr	Text
10 000		Computer sold - inflow of cash

In double entry bookkeeping the same post is also registered on an account for Sales, in credit:

SALES (REVENUE)		
Dr	Cr	Text
	10 000	Computer sold - increased revenue

Combined these two entries make up the total journal entry:

JOURNAL ENTRY – SALE OF COMPUTER			
Account	Dr	Cr	Text
Cash	10 000		Computer sold - inflow of cash
Sales		10 000	Computer sold - increased revenue

Normally there are four different **categories** of accounts:

1. Assets (balance account)
2. Liabilities (balance account)
3. Revenues (Income statement account)
4. Costs (Income statement account)

Assets can be cash, receivables, prepayments, machines and buildings. An increase in the value of an assets is recorded in debit and a decrease is recorded in credit.

Liabilities may be different types of payables or bank loans or loans from other credit institutions. An increase of a liability is recorded in credit and a liability reduction is recorded in debit.

Revenue normally corresponds to an inflow of assets and is recorded in credit. Costs normally correspond to a consumption of a resource and is recorded in debit.

Account no.	Account category	Debit (left)	Credit (right)
1	Assets (balance account)	↑ Increase	↓ Decrease
2	Equity and liabilities (balance accounts)	↓ Decrease	↑ Increase
3	Revenues (Income statement account)	↓ Decrease	↑ Increase
4	Costs (Income statement account)	↑ Increase	↓ Decrease

A journal entry in debit must always be matched by an equally large entry in credit which means that an increase in assets must always be matched by (1) a decrease of another asset or (2) an increase of a liability or (3) a cost reduction or (4) a revenue increase. An increase in liabilities must always be matched by (1) an increase of an asset or (2) a decrease of another liability or (3) a cost increase or (4) a revenue reduction, and so on in accordance to the table above.

A statement of all assets and liabilities at a given time is called a *balance sheet*. A statement of revenues and costs during a certain period is called an *income statement*. The difference between revenues and costs in a given period corresponds to the change in net assets (i.e. total assets minus total liabilities) during the period. If the revenues are greater than the costs, net assets has increased and if the costs are greater than revenues, net assets has decreased during the period.

APPENDIX 2:
INVENTORY AND ACCRUALS

INVENTORY:

An increase in the number and thus the total value of goods in stock in a producing worker council will generate a debit entry in the relevant sub account in account category *1.c.) Inventory*. A corresponding sub-account in account category *4.f) Social costs: accrual accounts -inventory* is credited. The social costs for the year is thereby reduced for the worker council.

INCREASE OF GOODS IN STOCK	
Dr	Cr
1.c) Inventory	4.f) Social costs: accruals account - inventory

A reduction in the number and thus the total value of goods in stock will generate a credit entry in the relevant sub account in account category *1.c.) Inventory*. The corresponding sub-account in account category *4.f) Social costs: accruals accounts -inventory* is debited. The social costs for the year is thereby increased for the worker council.

DECREASE OF GOODS IN STOCK	
Dr	Cr
4.f) Social costs: accrual accounts - inventory	1.c) Inventory

ACCRUALS:

Certain goods that are not classified as capital goods and are not kept in stock but have a value exceeding a certain amount and an economic lifespan in excess of a certain number of years may need to be accrued. It can be done through account *1.b) Accruals - Other goods*. The relevant sub account is debited at the time of acquisition by the acquisition cost, and account *1.a.) Available funds* is credited.

ACQUISITION OF GOODS WITH AN ECONOMIC LIFE > X YEARS	
Dr	Cr
1.b) Accruals - other goods	1.a) Available funds

Each period thereafter in the economic life of the good, the relevant sub account in account category 4.*g) Charged social costs: accrual accounts - inputs* is debited with the calculated depreciation amount. The correct sub account under *1.b) Accruals - other goods* is credited. This way the acquisition cost is accrued to the years in which the good is used.

PERIODIC DEPRECIATION OF INTERMEDIATE GOODS WITH AN ECONOMIC LIFE > X YEARS	
Dr	Cr
4.g) Social costs: accrual accounts- other goods	1.b) Accruals - other goods

APPENDIX 3:
ENTRIES FOR COLLECTIVE CONSUMER INVESTMENTS

At the time of a consumer councils' or federations' acquisition of a capital asset the correct cost centre for capacity costs is charged by the acquisition cost (A1).

COST CENTRE: CAPACITY COSTS - INVESTMENT	
Dr	Cr
A1. Investment Category - Acquisition cost investment	

The cost is then passed on to the consumer council or federation which made the investment decision. The cost centre is credited the acquisition cost (A2a)...

COST CENTRE: CAPACITY COSTS – DISTRIBUTION OF INVESTMENT COST TO THE COUNCIL OR FEDERATION	
Dr	Cr
	A2a. Transfer of acquisition cost investment

... and the accounting entity for the consumer council or federation is charged the same amount (A2b). The total acquisition cost for the investment is thus borne by the consumer council or federation.

CONSUMER COUNCIL - OR FEDERATION: INVESTMENT	
Dr	Cr
+ Other allocations of funds for collective consumption ...	+ Other allocations of funds for collective consumption ...
A2b. Investment Category	

The yearly depreciation amount for the investment, which normally is calculated by dividing the total acquisition cost with the economic life span, is charged to the cost centre *that handles the running operating costs* for production of the public service (B1). The depreciation cost will then be included in the operating costs passed on to members either via collective distribution or distribution via user fees.

COST CENTRE: RUNNING OPERATING COSTS - DEPRECIATION	
Dr	Cr
+ Other social costs ... B1. Depreciation	+ Allocation of costs to users via fees

If the annual depreciation cost of an investment is to be allocated collectively to the consumers, the depreciation cost can be charged to the consumer council or federation directly without having to go through the cost centre for running operating costs.

The same depreciation amount reduces the accounting rest value of the investment in the cost centre for capacity costs. The account for accumulated depreciation is credited by the depreciation amount (B2a). The same amount is then "repaid" to the consumer council or federation that made the investment so that the consumers as a collective will not be charged twice with the depreciation amount. The repayment is debited the cost centre for capacity costs (B2b) ...

COST CENTRE: CAPACITY COSTS - DEPRECIATION	
Dr	Cr
B2b. Repayments of funds to consumer council or federation	B2a. Accumulated depreciation -yearly depreciation

... and credited the consumer council or -federation that made the investment (B3).

CONSUMER COUNCIL OR - FEDERATION: DEPRECIATION	
Dr	Cr
+ Other allocations of funds for collective consumption ...	+ Transfer from individual consumers
	B3. Annual depreciation

REFERENCES AND LINKS

BOOKS

Anarchism – *Daniel Guerin, Monthly Review Press, 1970*

Financial Accounting, Principles and Issues. Third Edition – *Michael H. Granof, Prentice-Hall, 1985*

Micro Economics, Analysis & Policy. Fifth Edition – *Lloyd G. Reynolds, Irwin, 1985*

Liberating Theory – *Michael Albert et al, South End Press, 1986*

Macroeconomics – *Roger LeRoy Miller & Robert Pulsinelli, Harper & Row, 1986*

Relevance Lost; The Rise and Fall of Management Accounting – *H. Thomas Johnson & Robert S. Kaplan, Harvard Business School Press, 1987*

Produktkalkylering i omvandling – *Nils-Göran Olve & Lars A. Samuelsson, Mekanförbundet, 1989*

Looking forward – *Michael Albert & Robin Hahnel, South End Press, 1991*

The Political Economy of Participatory Economics – *Michael Albert & Robin Hahnel, Princeton University Press, 1991*

Parecon; Life after Capitalism – *Michael Albert, Verso, 2003*

On Anarchism – *Noam Chomsky, AK press, 2004*

Economic Justice and Democracy; From Competition to Cooperation – *Robin Hahnel, Routledge Books, 2005*

Realizing Hope; Life beyond capitalism – *Michael Albert, Zed Books, 2006*

Green Economics; Confronting the Ecological Crises – *Robin Hahnel, M.E. Sharp, 2011*

Of the People, By the People; The case for a Participatory Economy – *Robin Hahnel, Soapbox press, 2012*

The ABCs of Political Economy; A Modern Approach – *Robin Hahnel, Pluto Press, 2014*

Alternatives to Capitalism; Proposals for a Democratic Economy – *Robin Hahnel & Erik O. Wright, New Left Project, 2015*

ONLINE ARTICLES AND WEBSITES:

Monthly Review, 2008: Against the Market Economy: Advice to Venezuelan Friends:
www.monthlyreview.org/2008/01/01/against-the-market-economy-advice-to-venezuelan-friends

ZNet, 2010: Anarchist planning for the twenty first century:
www.zcomm.org/znetarticle/anarchist-planning-for-twenty-first-century-economies-a-proposal-by-robin-hahnel

Institute for Anarchist Studies: Anarchist Planning: An Interview with Robin Hahnel by Chris Spannos.:
www.anarchiststudies.mayfirst.org/node/432

New Politics, 2013: Of the People, By the People: Robin Hahnel interviewed by Stephen R. Shalom:
www.newpol.org/content/people-people

Participatory Economics: A Model for a New Economy 2014:
www.participatoryeconomics.info

Robin Hahnel's website:
www.robinhahnel.com

VIDEOS:

The Economic Choice beyond Capitalism and Communism:
www.youtube.com/watch?v=nbkDv0uidqE&feature=youtu.be.

Participatory Economics: Robin Hahnel:
www.youtube.com/watch?v=liqtfBmyQzA&list=PLghLjIYwg2cIXvomeFmY5M30HFgtEAuZS.

The Case against Markets:
www.youtube.com/watch?v=cUlefQePAd8&feature=youtu.be.

Robin Hahnel on Participatory Planning:
www.youtube.com/watch?v=TjJn0G2HLx0&feature=youtu.be.

ADVOCACY GROUPS:

Parecon Sverige:
www.parecon.se

Participatory Economics UK:
www.pe-uk.org

Parecon Finland
www.osallisuustalous.fi

Printed in Great Britain
by Amazon